Open Space Policy

Open Space Policy

New Jersey's Green Acres Program

Ronald A. Foresta

Rutgers University Press
New Brunswick, New Jersey

Library of Congress Cataloging in Publication
Data

Foresta, Ronald A., 1944–
  Open space policy.

  Bibliography: pp. 157–168
  Includes index.
  1. Open spaces—New Jersey.   2. Recrea-
tion areas—New Jersey.   I. Title.   II. Title:
Green Acres Program.
HT393.N5F67   333.78′4   81–2513
ISBN 0–8135–0923–8   AACR2

Contents

Maps and Figure

Maps

Figure

Tables

Acknowledgments

I would like to thank those whose suggestions, comments, and criticisms guided this work from its inchoate and not very promising beginnings to its present form. Thanks first and foremost to Susan Fainstein, who directed the dissertation out of which this book evolved. With her perception, critical skill, patience, and sometimes impatience, she managed to guide a difficult student through the rocks and whirlpools of thesis work. I have only just begun to realize the value of what she taught me. Thanks also to Robert Beauregard for his well-thought-out criticisms and especially for his organization suggestions that helped me solve the several structure problems that had me seriously checked. Michael Greenberg's perceptive reading of the manuscript led to several improvements; and Ken Mitchell's insightful comments, especially on the nature of bureaucratic politics in New Jersey, were also helpful. Also, I would like to thank Marion Clawson for his kind and encouraging reading of the manuscript and Paul Culhane, whose criticisms, both specific and general, were often painful but always constructive.

A note of thanks is also due to the Green Acres Program administrators who were so generous with their time and so patient with me. Without their unstinting help and active cooperation, this book would not have been possible.

Finally, I take all responsibility for any factual errors, misinterpretations, and canards found herein.

Open Space Policy

1

Introduction

On Election Day 1961, the voters of New Jersey made an important decision about the future of open space in the state. On the ballot was a public question that asked if a $60 million bond issue should be used to establish an ambitious program of acquiring public open space. The program would allow the state to acquire directly much park, forest, and game land. It would also permit the state to set up a local matching fund, out of which it could make grants to local governments for local acquisition of open space. The program, named the Green Acres Program, would transform New Jersey from a state with minimal, sporadic interest in public open space into one of those few whose commitment to public open space acquisition was active, ongoing, and expensive.

The referendum won handily, and soon a special state office was set up to run the Green Acres Program. The program, with funding from three subsequent bond issues, has been in continuous operation for almost two decades and has come to be widely viewed as the embodiment of the state's commitment to providing adequate open space within its borders. Over the years it has remained a highly visible program, so much so that in common parlance *Green Acres* has become a generic term meaning open spaces, parks, or forests of almost any ownership or status. The program is as popular as it is visible, both with the state's population and its officials. In operation the longest of any program of its kind in the nation, it is administered by a bureaucracy of professional administrators, planners, and land managers. It has spent or is authorized to spend over $.5 billion, making it one of the most expensive state open space programs in the nation.[1]

This is a case study of that program and of how a general state commitment to open space came to be condensed into specifics of policy, results, and benefits. To put the ambitions of this study into perspective, however, let me introduce a distinction that Lipset, Trow, and Coleman make. They divide case studies into two types according to their breadth of inference and their use of general laws. The first type of study uses *particularizing analysis*. In it, description and explanation of a single object or process is used "to provide information concerning its present state, and the dynamics through which it continues as it does." In this type of case study, understanding the immediate object of study is the sole goal. The second type uses *generalizing analysis*. Here, a case is used not for its own sake "but as an empirical basis either for generalization or theory construction."[2]

My study of the Green Acres Program is both particularizing and generalizing; for without being both, it could be neither. It is particularizing in the way it brings relevant general rules—for example, those governing bureaucratic behavior and interest-group tactics—to bear on an analysis of a particular entity, the Green Acres Program. The question that establishes the particularizing nature of my research task is a rather prosaic one: How are the resources allocated to the acquisition of public open space by the state of New Jersey distributed? In and of itself the question may be interesting to residents of New Jersey or to students of the workings of its government. National trends and the activities of other states enter the study in only two places. The first is in the exposition of the norms of public responsibility for providing open space, norms that informed New Jersey's behavior. The second is in a historical discussion of the programs of neighboring states that led to and served as models for the New Jersey program. Beyond this contextual information the study is overtly little concerned with open space beyond New Jersey's borders. It contains few comparisons of New Jersey's efforts with those of other states, surely too few for readers seeking an overview rather than an example of state-level open space preservation.

Yet many of the findings are applicable to states other than New Jersey. The Green Acres Program, because of its unequaled scale of funding and length of continued operation, makes an excellent laboratory for studying open space policy development. It is one of a large set of similar state programs; by 1977, twenty-three states had established bond-funded open space acquisition programs, and twenty-two had programs to help lower levels of government purchase tracts for recreation or conservation.[3] Thus, some of the study's conclusions and inferences will also apply to other programs that are, in their essentials, like New Jersey's. Furthermore, all states make some provision for the public acquisition of open space, and many face problems and dilemmas like those faced by New Jersey: Should proximity to population centers be an important acquisition consideration? Should open space policy be an instrument of state land-use control? Who should manage state open spaces and toward what ends—recreation, preservation, restraint of development? How New Jersey has dealt with these common questions is likely to be of interest beyond its borders.

The study also asks a broader question: What characteristics of public open space as a public good cause administrators, interest groups, and elected public officials to treat public space the way they do and, in so doing, make the pursuit of some goals easier than others and some outcomes more likely than others? For example, the state's planners exhibit biases toward providing certain kinds of open space, biases that appear to grow out of a professional ethic and a sense of mission not unique to New Jersey. Nor does their disregard for the practical problems of open space management stem from conditions found only there. The position of planners on open space matters would thus seem to be quite predictable from state to state and from one level of government to another. This, of course, is a generalizing matter. Using the case to study the interplay between such predispositions and the specifics of open space policy choices permits broader inferences about that interplay and formulation of general theories about government involvement in providing open space.

Finally, another path of inference and generalization leads across functional categories of public service. The decision-making process the study elucidates is in essence a planning process for meeting current and projected public needs through policy-forming decisions. Some of the lessons about bureaucratic behavior in meeting public open space needs are doubtlessly applicable to other areas of public interest involving similar problems and traditions of dealing with them, for example, resource conservation, maintenance of a high-quality environment, and the emerging field of amenity preservation.

The study is based on four separate but interrelated and sequential sets of questions, and the success of the study depends on answering each set in turn. The first set is historical and generative. How did the program come into being? What were the program's antecedents in other states and at other levels of government? These questions are important for two reasons. First, understanding the process that led to the program's establishment gives insights into the variety of interests in public open space not obtainable by looking at the program after it is established and routinized.[4] Second, examining the evolved norms and traditions of public responsibilities puts the Green Acres Program into a broad perspective and introduces many of the guidelines and conventions within which state decision makers work.

The second set, the policy set, is the center of this study. The policy questions elicit the process by which a general commitment produces tangible results. Among these questions are: Who with the Green Acres Program makes policy? What are the possible policy alternatives? What are the criteria on which policy is decided? What results and benefits have open space policy decisions delivered?

The third set is the environmental set. Public open space decision makers operate in an environment that includes members of the public, special interests directly affected by their actions, and those at the highest levels of state government with the ultimate responsibility for any decisions made under them. Here the questions asked are: What are the specific characteristics of the political environment in which state open space decisions are made? How do the attitudes and wishes of those affected by open space policy and those powerful in the state's political environment influence these decisions?

The final set of questions concerns evaluation, and perhaps these are the most important kinds of questions that can be asked about a policy process. Against what evaluative criteria should open space policy be judged? Then, having established these criteria, how does the Green Acres Program measure up?

The Historical Set

To set forth the structure and main themes of this work and introduce its data, secondary sources, and theoretical background, let me discuss these question sets in more detail. First, no public program or policy is created out of nothing, and the Green Acres Program was no exception. Although its establishment in 1961 appeared as a sudden, serious commitment where previously there had been none, many elements of that commitment had already been shaped by a long history of public involvement in the provision of open space and by traditions and norms that evolved within that history. The commitment was further shaped by the immediate events leading up to and surrounding the program's establishment.

Chapters 2 and 3 threat the historical questions, and in them a variety of sources are used. For the broad history of government involvement in open space, secondary sources on various aspects of public open space policy are useful, especially the massive final report of the Outdoor Recreation Resources Review Commissions, with its wealth of information on these matters.[5] Huth's and Nash's treatments of the evolution of federal concern for the great national open spaces are also of great help, as is Knapp's detailed survey of public concern for urban open spaces.[6] For the narrower question of open space policy in New Jersey before Green Acres, the irregular series of open space planning reports issued by various New Jersey planning agencies from the 1930s on and the reports of the Regional Plan Association are important.[7] They offered enough data and interpretation to piece together a detailed picture of the sporadic bouts of state concern for open space before 1961. For the immediate circumstances surrounding the establishment of the Green Acres Program, I rely most heavily on interviews with the principals, their meeting minutes, and their correspondence. Although I found some disagreement among the sources on a few points, the main points as presented here do not involve choosing from conflicting sources.

Chapter 2 treats the origins of government involvement in public open space and shows how a distinct, if somewhat unsettled, role for the states evolved only after the federal government and local governments had long been actively providing for public open space. This chapter also treats the various traditions and norms of state responsibility that evolved along with increasing state involvement in public open space. Chapter 3, turning specifically to New Jersey, examines the state's open space activities before the advent of the Green Acres Program and shows how those activities reflected the wider traditions and patterns discussed in the preceding chapter. It continues with a discussion of the immediate events leading up to the Green Acres Program; and in so doing, it identifies the principal open space policy actors and introduces many of the themes developed in subsequent chapters. The chapter closes with a discussion of the formal structure of the program's policy-making apparatus as originally established and subsequently modified.

The Policy Set

The policy questions—Who makes policy decisions? On what criteria are they made, toward what ends, and to what effect? To what degree is policy conformant with the models and norms of open space responsibility delineated in Chapter 2?—are addressed through several distinct literatures. First, there is the large body of writing on public open space. Unfortunately, from the viewpoint of the policy analyst, most of it is normative and advocatory, and most of its writers have been primarily concerned with arguing for changes in the status quo. Aside from this activist orientation, there are few unifying threads within this literature. Instead there are wide differences both in concerns and in the philosophical biases underlying the analyses and the arguments.

The actual or adopted literati of the wilderness movement, including Marshall, Muir, Stegner, and MacKaye among the most prominent, are one group of such normative writers.[8] Their arguments for public acquisition and preservation of vast wilderness tracts grow out of a rejection of basic aspects of modern civilization and perhaps even out of a certain misanthropy. Another, more disparate group is primarily concerned with urban open spaces. It includes the nineteenth-century landscape architects such as Burnham and Olmsted, who argued that city open space was necessary for the health and aesthetic satisfaction of its citizens.[9] It also includes those who, like McHarg and Niering, consider urban open space necessary for the preservation of natural processes on which the city's environmental health depends.[10] Still others such as Lynn, Chapin, and Whyte have advocated increased use of public open space to channel urban development along rational, efficient lines.[11]

Perhaps surprisingly, the interest in public open space evidenced by all these groups has prompted relatively few analytic studies of government open space policy making, and most of these few are concerned with the management of federal lands. Schiff, for example, looks at the way Forest Service administrators responded to new scientific information with implications for fire-fighting policy. Ise examines the evolution of national park management principles; Harry, Gale, and Hendee look at decision making concerning wilderness. Dana and Peffer look at federal policies concerned with grazing on the public domain and the use of the national forests. Nienaber and Wildavsky study the relationship between the budget process and land management in the National Park Service.[12]

There are very few studies of public open space acquisition per se. Taken together, they may mislead the unsuspecting analyst of public acquisition policy by their almost exclusive concern with the interplay of private interest groups. Such a concern seems to be an inevitable outgrowth of what the students of open space acquisition politics usually choose to study: the occasional highly visible conflict surrounding the future of particular tracts of land. As Lowi points out, where there is, in a political arena, a discrete, visible prize that is not readily divisible and does not lend itself to accommodation through compromise, there will be interest groups in active confrontation.[13] Such is the nature of the prize in most case studies of open space politics; such is the nature of the politics the studies illuminate.

In these studies, government is usually portrayed as a passive actor. A unit of government becomes involved in the issue well after the array of interests is articulated and the conflict has broken out. Its role is largely adjudicative; it decides in favor of one of the sides or it uses its resources to force a compromise that, without its sovereign intervention, would not have been possible. Platt's study, *The Open Space Decision Process*, illustrates this genre. Each of the four cases of conflict he examines begins with a "crisis": an owner wants to develop a privately held tract of undeveloped land that others use or appreciate in its undeveloped state. This leads to a reactive mobilization of those who have an interest in the preservation of the tract. The lines are drawn, the battle is joined, and ultimately the government is drawn in. In the end, the government exercises sovereignty and either thwarts the developer through preemptive acquisition or permits him to proceed, thus ending the conflict. Similarly, both Tannenbaum and Strong, who examined the processes of open space preservation in New York and Pennsylvania respectively, chose to look at highly visible conflicts that government entered primarily to negotiate between conflicting interests.[14] In the end it made decisions that were little more than capitulations to the strongest external pressures. Recently Grabber has attempted to show that many federal wilderness decisions are the result of intense pressure brought on federal officials by a small group of relatively skilled, uncompromising wilderness activists.[15]

Not all government activity, however, is adjudicative, passive, and exposed to such conflict and pressure. In fact, it is probable that little of the public business involves the overt interest-group conflict that students of open space politics have chosen to study. Bachrach and Baratz, Sharkansky, and Lowi have all demonstrated the importance of political processes in which routinization and consensus rather than crisis and conflict are the salient characteristics.[16]

The bulk of research on government involvement in the preservation of open space notwithstanding, New Jersey's involvement in open space acquisition through the Green Acres Program is highly routinized and has been largely nonconflictual. Although open space is a public issue with much potential for conflict, and New Jersey is no exception, the Green Acres Program has usually avoided controversy. It is structurally insulated from some areas of conflict by its chartering provisions, and it is steered clear of other areas by the skill of its administrators. The state normally becomes involved in local grants-in-aid acquisitions only after any local-level conflict has been resolved, although it is the occasional exceptions that attract much media and popular attention. Public open space acquisitions by the state as part of government-imposed settlements of conflict have been few; most state acquisitions have been the result of bureaucratic initiatives or of state follow-ups on private offerings. Government decisions to purchase or not to purchase have for the most part been in keeping with long-range plans and policies formulated within the bureaucracy itself.

Such ongoing programs are clearly in a world of open space acquisition politics different from that normally examined. At its center are the professional recreation specialist, the land manager, the wildlife biologist, and the career public administrator. Understanding it depends on understanding the rules by which public bureaucracies work. Weber; Downs; and Simon, Smithburg, and Thompson—basic theorists in the area of public administration and bureaucratic dynamics—are trusty guides here; and to a more limited extent, so are Pressman and Wildavsky and Dunshire. Because we are dealing with a distinct type of bureaucracy, one which distributes a public good, Levy, Meltsner, and Wildavsky; Lineberry; and Jones are especially helpful.[17] Each examines systems of distributing public benefits that are similar to the Green Acres Program in that they are what Jones calls *closed systems*. Within closed systems, distributive procedures are mostly decided by a public bureaucracy free from specific pressures from without and little influenced by immediate political considerations.

Understanding the world of open space acquisition politics also requires understanding the unique characteristics of open space that predispose public officials to deal with it in certain ways and to prefer providing it in certain forms and certain places. Although the open space administrator is removed from most of the interests that motivate the better understood actors in open space politics—desire for personal use, nostalgia, concern for the local tax base—he does not lack biases or interests. He is far from being the bureaucratic automaton of the Webernian stereotype.[18] As Blau, Downs, and others show, public officials act from all sorts of motives—desire for security, ambition, frustration, a sense of professionalism, even idealism—to influence policy in its formulation and to modify it in its execution.[19] Open space is an area of government activity rich in opportunities for building empires, stroking egos, securing careers, and giving vent to idealistic impulses. It also contains its own snags and obstacles waiting to damage the reputation of an agency or the career of an administrator.

Open space as an object of public administration has been little explored, which is not surprising really. Neither the normative literature on open space nor even the corpus of research on open space politics point in that direction. Nevertheless, understanding the opportunities and dangers open space acquisition presents to civil servants, and how they respond to them, is central to understanding open space policy making and the process by which public open space has become an important part of our landscape.

This part of my study has proved to be the most complex and in many ways the most difficult. There are no models to help with research organization and there is no body of theoretical literature on open space policy making to provide a context for the findings. Interviews with present and former state officials and, for the local matching fund, with county and local officials were invaluable sources of information on actual procedures and decision criteria, as were the minutes of various state committees concerned with public open space. Policy directives and public policy statements from the agencies that took part in decision making were useful, and newspapers provided some valuable case material. The files of the State Department of Environmental Protection were my primary source of data on tracts acquired and amounts spent, the data used in analyzing the program results.

These questions of policy formation are treated in Chapters 4 and 5. Because the structure and dynamics of the state's direct acquisition program and its local matching program are so different, a separate chapter is devoted to each. In Chapter 4, I discuss the advantages and disadvantages to the program's decision makers of pursuing the various acquisition policies open to them. Then I explore the reasons for the evolution within the stage acquisition program of a policy strongly favoring large rural acquisitions. Chapter 5 looks at the policy making and administration of the local matching fund. Here, discussion centers on what has led the program's administrators to allow policy making to be diffused among the state's local governments. This in turn leads to an examination of the local conditions responsible for the differing program participation rates of various types of counties and municipalities.

The Environmental Set

The third set of questions, on the political environment within which the state's open space administrators work, is treated in Chapter 6. The most important and interesting of these questions is why those outside the state bureaucracy with the formal and actual power to influence open space policy strongly infrequently do so, allowing instead the decisions made by the bureaucracy to be most prominent in determining open space policy.

It would be natural to assume that Green Acres policy and results would be determined by the organized interest groups that figure so prominently in visible open space politics. The conditions seem right for the output dualism that Edelman found in public regulatory agencies: symbols and sop to an uncritical public and substantive benefits to a knowing and politically skilled interest group.[20] With open space provision, as with industry regulation, there is a public whose support for the government activity in question is not coupled with much critical scrutiny. Likewise, there are organized interests who would materially benefit from the choice of one policy and its results over another. In fact, Graber and Stillman both postulate that such symbolic obfuscation and subversion of public interest by private groups is a central characteristic of open space politics.[21]

The Green Acres Program has not, however, been captured by organized interests. Notwithstanding superficial parallels between open space and regulatory politics, important differences exist. With public open space programs there is seldom the simple dichotomized choice between interest serving and public serving that seems to prevail in the regulatory activities examined by Edelman. Seldom is one private interest group pitted against a clear-cut public interest with a corresponding choice of policies that would favor one or the other. Instead, there is usually a multiplicity of possible acquisition policies all arguably in the public interest, and seldom is there a predominant private interest, or phalanx of interests, behind any particular policy. This is not to say that there are no private, organized interest groups in the arena of public open space policy in New Jersey. There certainly are, and they run the gamut from the Cranberry Growers Association to the Friends of Animals. With few exceptions, however, they have neither the political skills nor the muscle nor the unity of interest to define policy consistently in their favor. Put simply, extragovernmental groups are ephemeral (although occasionally important) determinants of state open space policy.

Like the state's organized interest groups, its elected state officials have little de facto influence on the course of open space policy. Although the legislature and the governor must approve the legislation that authorizes open space spending, they do so routinely. For the most part they do not regard open space as an important issue requiring much of their time; they are content to leave policy matters to administrators. Even when they occasionally do show interest in policy, that interest is neither deep enough nor sustained enough to force changes on a reluctant bureaucracy settled into its own preferred ways.

For the attitudes and influence of the state's interest groups, my study relies primarily on interviews with spokesmen for the groups and with state administrators who have dealings with them. Bentley and Truman, basic theorists of interest group dynamics, were important in helping me frame questions about the influence of such groups on open space policies; but Lowi and Bauer, Poole, and Dexter, with their discussions of the causes of interest group inactivity and ineffectiveness in certain political arenas, provided the keys to understanding what I found when I examined the decision process.[22]

Most difficult to explain was the great gap between the formal power of the legislature and the governor and their actual influence on policy. My study relies on the text of legislation, legislative directives, executive orders, and press releases to delineate the formal power. The opinions of the elected officials themselves, as well as those of the open space administrators, were most important in understanding the degree of influence. Several authors were important in explaining what I observed. Redford and Freeman were valuable for their analyses of the interaction between public administrators and legislators. Long and Rourke were both helpful in explaining the bases of a public agency's power to resist demands made on it from the outside. Fox's treatment of the relationships of public bureaucracies to the public, Dye's discussion of the real limits of executive power, and Lee's essay on legislative decision making stand out as important in bridging the gap between the great formal powers of elected public officials and their minimal direct policy influence.[23]

The Evaluative Set

The fourth set of questions concerns evaluation. Identification of the key elements in the formulation of public policy or explanation of the conversion process by which a general public responsibility becomes concrete results are in themselves seldom satisfactory ends of public policy research. They seem to lead naturally to value judgments. Evaluation questions always arise in dealing with government activity involving a range of potential policies, each with a unique array of tangible benefits and associated beneficiaries. Are the policies formulated and the benefits produced the optimal ones, or even satisfactory ones? Are they worth the opportunity costs in options foregone and goods and services not delivered? Such questions compel judgments. Although $.5 billion is a lot of money to spend on open space in a state of 7,000 square miles, it is not nearly enough to acquire all the open space for which strong arguments for acquisition can be made. Hence, open space is a scarce resource. One tract purchased means another not purchased or its purchase postponed. One set of ends pursued means others ignored. One set of benefits bestowed means another set foregone.

Altshuler; Lineberry; and Levy, Meltsner, and Wildavsky all address the problem of evaluating the outcomes of public policy making in such diverse areas as city planning, police and fire protection, street paving, and the provision of education.[24] Unfortunately, as their studies taken together show, evaluation of a process that distributes a public good must be based to a considerable degree on the unique characteristics of that good itself. Thus few of their evaluative criteria were transferable to my study, and evaluating New Jersey's open space policies meant formulating as well as applying suitable criteria.

Because public open space policy can be used in the pursuit of widely disparate goals, policy evaluations are always in danger of becoming mired down in problems of apples versus oranges. For example, how does one weigh the lost recreation opportunities of a policy that maximizes the preservation of unique ecological systems? Or how does one decide if the use of open space funds in the service of development planning in the suburbs was worth the opportunity costs of not acquiring spectacular, if remote, scenic areas? These are difficult if not unanswerable questions. Fortunately, circumstances mitigated such problems in connection with the Green Acres Program. First, New Jersey's open space policy stressed environmental considerations at the same time it was pursuing recreational ends. Second, although open space policy was not used to further rational, state-level land use planning, any policy shifts in this direction would undoubtedly under the circumstances have been ineffective. Hence, a happy confluence of goals on the one hand and a lack of real opportunity costs on the other narrowed the wide and perhaps unmanageable range of possible evaluation criteria down to the two categories of citizen access and quality of the accessible open space provided. Ultimately, I came to concentrate my evaluation on the question of who benefits most from the goods and services provided by the Green Acres Program; and in so doing, I placed myself in the camp of those policy analysts who are most concerned with equality of distribution.

A major problem immediately arose with this course of evaluation, that of selecting a critical distance and focus. Should I stand at great distance and be critical of the state's open space policies because of their failure to do much to correct the enormous inequality of landscape amenity and habitability created by a century and a half of laissez-faire industrial economy? Or should I adopt a narrower perspective, dismiss such failures as absolutely inevitable, and judge the program for what it has done within the few degrees of freedom that socioeconomic and political circumstances have allowed it? Abandoning the broad view would mean ignoring the enormity of inequality within which an open space program must operate, an inequality that behaves like a gray eminence, quietly inhibiting certain policies while encouraging others. With the broad view one sees the way in which the powerful benefit from the operation of the program. Similarly one sees the ways in which the program perpetuates the social and economic status quo. Surely an open space policy should aim at reducing this; yet at times a narrow view must be adopted. Failure to do so would mean losing an opportunity to evaluate the program against any realistic assessment of its potential and would cast a pall of nihilism over its achievements.

In judging the Green Acres Program and New Jersey's open space policy in Chapter 7, I try to adopt both perspectives by subjecting the Green Acres outcomes to three interrelated and succeedingly more demanding criteria. The first is geographic. Has the program's distribution of benefits made open space reasonably accessible to all geographic segments of the state's population? The findings suggest that the answer is yes. The second criterion is one of use. Has the state's open space policy engendered a pattern of use whereby all the broad geographic and socioeconomic groupings of the state's citizens take advantage of open space? Here too the answer seems to be yes. A final criterion is based on popular values. Has state policy led to the provision of the kinds of open space that people most value? The answer appears to be no. From these yesses and nos must come suggestions for changing what is found wanting and strengthening what is of value. The final section is devoted to a discussion of the possibility of, and the responsibility for, closing the gap between the open spaces the state's residents want and those their government provides.

Perhaps a final note on perspective and definition is in order here at the closing of the introduction. For its students, public policy is topologically rich terrain; one question seems to lead at once to half a dozen others. Unfortunately, this means that isolating public policy questions, and thereby defining a research problem, involves cutting what seem like natural threads of inquiry. Questions are inevitably raised, or at least hinted at, and then passed over. This book is no exception; it raises and suggests more questions than it answers, but this is probably how it should be.

2

Open Space and the Role of the State

By the time New Jersey committed itself to an active open space policy with the establishment of the Green Acres Program in 1961, the American states had been involved in providing public open space for more than fifty years. Over those years precedents had accumulated so that a niche of state responsibility had evolved between those of the national and local governments. As this niche evolved, however, much remained unclear and unsettled. Most important was the ambiguity about where state responsibility ended and that of other levels of government began: Furthermore, two distinct and somewhat dissonant models of state responsibility toward its citizens developed. Both matters were to become the principal points of policy conflict in New Jersey. Let me trace the evolution of the states' role in the provision of open space and attempt to identify the models of state responsibility that evolved along with it. To do this, I must first show how other levels of government became involved with public open space and the forms this involvement took.

The Municipal Role

Although the provision of open space is not a function assigned by law to a specific level of government, the nineteenth century saw parks, forests, and public open lands become the subject of great interest at the municipal and federal levels. Municipal responsibility for providing public open space had its antecedents in the history of the world's great cities. The provision of piazzas, promenades, and public gardens was an accepted civic responsibility in Europe from the Renaissance on, and these traditions of urban open space persisted in the layout of colonial American cities—Savannah and Philadelphia being two of the better examples of colonial open space planning. Unfortunately, the task of coping with the explosive growth of American cities in the early nineteenth century left little civic energy available for providing public open spaces, and they were by and large omitted from the tissue of urban expansion.[1] By mid-century, however, urban parks were becoming an object of public concern. Tannenbaum writes of New York that by the 1850s the proposal to develop Central Park had become a key issue in city politics, even to the point of contributing heavily to the election of a propark mayor.[2] The following decades saw open space become an important issue in other major cities such as Boston, Chicago, Buffalo, and San Francisco.[3]

Once public open space did enter civic consciousness, there arose numerous and distinct rationales (most still current) for providing it. One had to do with health; both folk wisdom and the prevailing transcendental thought of the era ascribed great benefits to contact with nature. "City for wealth, country for health" was typical nineteenth-century conventional wisdom.[4] It was partly to benefit public health that Horace Greeley crusaded indefatigably for the establishment of Central Park, a preserved patch of country to serve as the lungs of the city and as an antidote for the miasmic poisons of its crowded residential districts. In the nineteenth century, sunlight and the circulation of fresh air were in and of themselves thought to have curative powers. Olmsted, the creator of Central Park, subscribed to this theory and cited with pride the ruined constitutions restored to vigor by a brief daily carriage ride in the parks he designed.[5] Mental and social health entered into the rationale for municipal provision of open spaces as progressive philanthropy came to see local parks and play areas as a preventive for juvenile delinquency bred by boredom and the general conditions of the crowded urban districts.[6]

The uses of public open space to channel and direct urban growth and to eliminate unsavory or unsanitary land uses were espoused early by park planners. In the nineteenth century, the development of riparian parks often conveniently rid their sites of the squatter settlements that lined urban watercourses. Olmsted was aware of the connection between human residence or industry near rivers and the pollution of their waters.[7] Because of this connection he suggested as a general rule of city planning that waterways should be protected from such degradation by reserving their banks as parks. Thus, it was partly for what we would today call ecological considerations that Olmsted's great metropolitan park systems relied heavily on stream valleys and river frontage.

Those involved in planning the late nineteenth-century city were also aware of the aesthetic and symbolic uses of open spaces; Olmsted advocated park systems to distinguish a city from others, to give it individuality, and to serve as a source of municipal pride.[8] His park designs capitalized as much as possible on unique natural landscape features. For Montreal this meant the preservation, as a great park, of the mountain around which the city was built and after which it was named. For Boston he advocated both sweeping expanses of meticulously maintained greenswards and formally laid out public promenades—for personal pleasure to be sure, but equally for the image and reputation of the city. Indeed, in the late nineteenth century one of the necessary ornaments of a great American city was a park system designed by one of the great landscape architects, preferably Olmsted himself. For Chicago one of the marks of its arrival as a great city was a municipal open space system that included a spectacular riverfront park inset with spare-no-expense public buildings in the best beaux arts tradition of the period and a fairground sufficient to hold the mammoth Columbian Exposition of 1892/93.

For cities of the nineteenth century the philanthropic interest of the very wealthy was important in turning civic aspirations into open spaces. The very rich often served as park commissioners, dipping into their own funds to further commission aims when government was reluctant or unable to supply public money and often making large donations of land from their private holdings to public park systems. Harriman Park in New York's Orange and Rockland counties and much of the Cook County Forest Reserve in suburban Chicago came to be public land through the activities and donations of the very rich.

In summary, by the late nineteenth century the municipal role in the provision of open space was well established. Most of the great American cities, prompted by Olmsted and members of the city beautiful movement, had greatly expanded their public open spaces. Municipal governments and private philanthropists laid out large sums for the acquisition and development of park systems, usually including a central park, several subsidiary ones, and perhaps serpentine parkways or broad esplanades to bind the elements together into an interconnected network of green places. Such park systems came to be accepted as one of the public facilities, like sewers, water supply systems, and street lights, that a large city government was expected to supply.[9] In thousands of smaller cities and towns throughout the nation, scaled-down versions of the great municipal parks appeared— small central parks with their bandstands in a formal setting compactly juxtaposed against pastoral landscapes in miniature.[10]

The Federal Role

While the municipal role in providing public open space was evolving, so was that of the federal government. As Elson shows, in the nineteenth century the great natural places such as Grand Canyon and Niagara Falls had great symbolic significance for a people without Europe's wealth of historic or cultural artifacts to fix upon as symbols of national identity.[11] The idea of the federal government as the logical keeper of these special natural features came up again and again. In the 1830s, the artist Catlin went so far as to propose that the great plains, complete with its herds of bison and its nomadic Indians, be set aside as a vast national park.[12] He proposed a park running from the eastern edge of the short-grass prairies to the Rocky Mountain Front. It would serve as a source of national identity and pride. In it, flora, fauna, and indigenous culture alike would be preserved and protected from the depredations of white American agriculture, buffalo hunting, whiskey, and trade goods. According to Olmsted, access to the great natural places was an essential for the pursuit of happiness; as such, the federal government had the same responsibility for making it available as it had for insuring life and liberty.[13] He believed that, without government action, access to nature would be preempted by the rich to the exclusion of the rest of society.[14]

Out of the activities of such park advocates as Freemont and Olmsted and the favorable public response they elicited came the national park movement and, in 1872, Yellowstone, the first national park. In the next decades there was a steady accumulation of national parks until, in 1916, they were unified under the National Park Service. Once accepted, the premise that the federal government had a responsibility to preserve special natural places was never again seriously questioned.

The late nineteenth century also saw the national forest system established and gradually enlarged. It was concern for the nation's timber and mineral resources that led the federal government to declare parts of the public domain national forest. The alienation of these forests from public ownership was prohibited, and ostensibly their future use was to be subject to strict regulation according to the principles of conservation. Shortly after World War I, the management of national forests for recreation joined management for resource conservation. The influence of Aldo Leopold, whose writing popularized the notion of land management according to ecological principles, combined with the rising demand to use the national forests for contact with nature coming from an increasingly mobile population, led to the establishment of primitive and roadless areas within the forests. These were areas where logging was prohibited, ecological cycles were allowed to proceed undisturbed, and personal enjoyment was encouraged.[15]

In the first years of the twentieth century came the establishment of the National Wildlife Refuge System. Pelican Island, the first refuge, was established in 1902 and was soon followed by many others. Shortly after the establishment of the refuge system, federal concern for ecological integrity led to the passage of the important Weeks Act of 1911. With this act, Congress authorized the U.S. Forest Service to purchase watershed land and add it to the public domain, where it would be protected from any development that would impair its water- and soil-retention capacities. The forest service thus moved from the passive management of open space in the public domain to its active acquisition.[16]

So by the early twentieth century, federal as well as municipal governments had been deeply involved in provision and preservation of open space for many decades and had accumulated a range of rationales for this involvement: health and enjoyment of the citizenry, protection of natural resources, preservation of sacred places, and maintenance of ecological integrity. In contrast, the states, with some isolated exceptions, had no role in, nor sense of responsibility for, providing public open space until well into the twentieth century.

Conflicting Models of State Responsibility

State interest in open land through most of the nineteenth century was usually aimed at getting it into private hands and onto local tax roles as developed property. In the East, states faced a continual problem of lands being sold to private individuals, being exploited for their resources or made the object of speculative venture, and ultimately winding up in the public domain again for nonpayment of taxes.

During the closing decades of the nineteenth century, however, many states followed the federal example and established state forests, into which they put the relapsed land. In most states these forests served as public hunting lands. Some states set up demonstration areas in their forests where they attempted to show private landowners the benefits of scientific woodland management.[17] Several decades before the Weeks Act, New York State banned tree cutting on state land in the Adirondacks and authorized the state to buy back

Adirondack land that had previously been sold from the public domain. The state's primary purpose was to maintain the water-retaining capacities of the Adirondack slopes by insuring that their vegetative cover remained intact.[18]

In the East, Pennsylvania and New York had established small state parks by the mid-nineteenth century, Valley Forge and Washington Crossing Parks in Pennsylvania and Niagara Falls Park in New York. These were parks that had their genesis in the desire to extend state protection to special historic or natural sites. Farther west, Michigan acquired Fort Mackinac as a park, and later in the century Yosemite Valley was transferred from the federally managed public domain to the state of California. The first state park system was established in Iowa in 1918 when that state pulled its disparate open space holdings together under one centralized management.

The federal government actively encouraged the development of state open space facilities, and to this end, the first National Conference of State Park Commissioners was held under the aegis of the National Park Service in 1921. Now that the auto was increasing mobility and the use of open spaces previously inaccessible to most people, the federal government saw state parks as a means of relieving its own facilities of some of the pressure of popular demand (a pressure that had just forced the forest service to shift its management principles toward recreation) and also as a means of serving regions of the country where national facilities were scarce, notably the East and Midwest. The federal government also saw an important role for the states in preserving the hundreds of natural areas whose acquisition and management were, collectively, beyond federal financial capability.[19] The states responded by quickening their pace of acquisition.

Thus, in the early twentieth century the states were increasingly drawn into responsibility for providing public open space. Two somewhat contradictory roles evolved out of the accumulated traditions of state provision of open public places. To understand these roles it is necessary to consider some of the characteristics of open space as a public good.

As a general rule for public open spaces, size, remoteness, degree of development, and intensity of use are highly correlated. At one extreme are the large open spaces used for escape into wilderness, places where ecological systems proceed undisturbed, far from the routine, the materialism, and the consumer values of urban civilization. At the other extreme are the small, intensively used open spaces in the middle of urban activity, open space whose use is not complete escape but socialization or momentary respite. Between the extremes fall the grand urban parks, founded on the faith of Olmsted and others that the simulated pastoral had a great salutary effect on the city dweller. Also in the spectrum are easily accessible rural areas such as those valued by Henry David Thoreau as so necessary for striking the proper balance of the tame and the wild, both on the landscape and within the psyche.

By removing these open space types from the contexts of social, environmental, and personal philosophy in which they were initially proposed and combining them as elements in an open space system, an ideal open space landscape can be created, one synchronized both with the phased cycles of American middle-class life and with American traditions of assigning fiscal public responsibility. For daily living there are the *user-oriented open spaces,* the small, proximate, intensively used open spaces. Their virtues lie mostly in their accessibility and their user orientation. Clawson and Knetsch perhaps best describe these places: "All the parks, playgrounds, and similar areas within the city, and most of them nearby, are 'user-oriented,' in our terminology. That is, their location is determined primarily, and sometimes within very narrow tolerances, by where people live and work. Such areas are designed to be used daily, during clement weather, although they may get a heavier use on weekends than on other days."[20] At the other end of the spectrum are *resource-based open spaces:* "Their dominant characteristic is their outstanding physical resources. . . . The major areas of this type are mountains, desert, sea, and lake shores, and swamps—areas that usually lie at considerable distance from concentrations of population. . . . Except for the historical sites, which are often small, most resource-based outdoor recreation areas are fairly large units, generally of several thousand acres or more."[21] These are also the annual vacation open spaces, usually the goal of a major travel undertaking.

In the nineteenth century the user-oriented places were accessible by urban transit to the group most able to articulate demands for open space, the middle class of the cities. By the later decades of the century, the resource-oriented places were accessible to these same people by the nation's railroads. The advent of the automobile made the intermediate places—what Clawson calls *regional open space*—accessible, too. Such intermediate open spaces are neither wholly resource oriented nor completely user oriented in location; both site and situational qualities are of some importance here. These are the weekend open spaces; they fit into the third, intermediate cycle of American life, the weekly one.

Such a hierarchy of open spaces lends itself to a logical assignment of government responsibilities. For local, user-oriented places, with the user group drawn from the immediate surrounding area, responsibility seems to fall naturally to the lowest level of jurisdiction, the municipal government. The responsibility for the great places, because of their national symbolic importance, the national user population they draw, or the national significance of the environmental resources they represent, seems to fall naturally to the federal government. The intermediate places, then, are the logical responsibility of the intermediate levels of government, the states and, to a lesser extent, their creatures, the counties.

Such a hierarchy also fits the distribution of costs to the distribution of benefits. Local parks, drawing mostly local users and containing natural resources of local importance, are paid for out of local taxes. County parks, drawing their users from within the county and of environmental benefit to the county, are paid for out of county revenues. Proceeding up the hierarchy of open spaces, both the area to which benefits are distributed and the area over which expenses are borne expand.

Such a hierarchy of responsibility is appealing in its crispness and clarity of assignment, so much so that it is amenable to presentation in chart form. In fact, Clawson, Held, and Stoddard have drawn up a table that matches general location of the open spaces, activities for which they are appropriate, their size, and their period of use with the level of government responsible for their provision.[22]

In practice things are not so simple. First, when this hierarchy is applied to open space managed primarily for conservation rather than recreation, those receiving the benefits, and thus the corresponding locus of responsibility, is usually not clear. But more important, there are strong traditions of interaction, coordination, and compensatory provision of open space among levels of government that further obscure responsibilities. For one, there has always been downward movement of information, money, and sometimes even land titles from the federal government to lower levels. From their very inception, the National Park Service and the U.S. Forest Service served as models for state forest and park agencies. Stephen Mather, the first director of the National Park Service, established an office of liaison for dissemination of information and advice to state governments, and as mentioned above, the National Park Service sponsored the first National Conference of State Park Commissioners. When the National Park Service was offered a property deemed not suitable for inclusion in the National Park System yet suitable for a state park, it would alert the state and do everything possible to help it acquire the property if it wished to.

In the 1930s, the federal government bought many tracts of land under its submarginal land program, developed them for recreation or conservation with Civilian Conservation Corps (CCC) labor, and turned them over to the states for inclusion in their park and forest systems. Often, CCC labor was used to upgrade recreation facilities in state parks or forests, and most states had park management and recreation plans drawn up for them by the National Park Service. Furthermore, facilities constructed by the Bureau of Reclamation and the Army Corps of Engineers are frequently turned over to local or state governments for recreational purposes, as are federal properties deemed surplus by the General Services Administration.[23] The federal government also makes available through various programs grant funds for state open space acquisitions. The most important of these federal programs have been the Department of Housing and Urban Development's programs to improve urban environments, including the community block grant program, and the Bureau of Outdoor Recreation's Land and Water Conservation Fund, which funds a wide range of state and local projects in urban and rural areas.[24]

A tradition of intergovernment arrangements for the provision of public open space also exists among state, county, and local governments. Many states have programs under which state lands can be turned over to lower levels of government for use as parks, and many states provide their counties and municipalities with professional advice in acquiring, developing, or maintaining open space. Many also complement this advice with financial aid programs. Although grants from the Land and Water Conservation Fund go from the federal government to local governments, states have the right to set guidelines for applications for these funds from their counties and municipalities. The state thus acts as an intermediary.

Sometimes circumstances have rendered lower levels of government incapable of providing adequate open space and have led the states to create special-purpose government units with unique areal jurisdiction, for example, the Palisades Interstate Park Commission with bistate (New York and New Jersey) jurisdiction within the New York metropolitan area.[25] Similarly, Massachusetts has established special park districts that encompass most of its larger urban centers and their surrounding areas, thus cutting across established municipal and county boundaries.

Although the county, like the state, has a discrete level of responsibility in the hierarchial scheme of open space responsibility, the first county park systems were established at least in part to compensate for lower level failures. The turn of the twentieth century saw the establishment of the nation's first county park commissions in urbanized northern New Jersey, but organization and in the ends served, they were very much like the municipal park commissions of large cities. These early county park commissions responded to a need for centralized open space planning not possible under fragmented territorial authority on the municipal level, and the park systems they created were essentially urban.

Open space systems are often found in complementary relationships in which vigor at one level of government seems to encourage inactivity at other levels. In New York's Westchester County, with one of the best county park systems in the country, the state's regional park commission has been virtually inactive. In neighboring Orange and Rockland counties, where the Palisades Interstate Park Commission has long been active and has major holdings, county park systems long remained underdeveloped.[26]

This complementarity and overlapping of roles has probably been encouraged by the professionalization of those fields of public administration that touch on open space. This professionalization has encouraged the easy circulation of open space personnel among local, county, state, and federal agencies and created a general awareness and sympathy among administrators for problems found at other levels. Professional meetings are frequently used to "preclear" ideas and to sound out associates on one level of government on programs or policy changes being contemplated at another level.[27] The net result has undoubtedly been a blurring of the lines of responsibility and an increasing flexibility in defining the role of any particular level of government.

Hierarchy and Intervention

Thus, two traditions in government provision of open space developed while the states were adding open space to the range of public goods for which they were responsible. The first tradition, with its exclusive assignment of open space responsibilities to the various levels of government, incorporated an elegant stratified, or *hierarchical model*. Most public open space activity probably has in fact been in keeping with this model. The sheer practicality of local provision of locally used parks and county, state, and federal provision of open spaces for wider use and benefit is usually compelling. Nevertheless, there always has been the crossing of the lines in the interactive tradition. It is a tradition with a much less clear allocation of responsibility and a much less elegant justification; in fact Grodzins referred to it as "a chaos of responsibility."[28] The presence of special acquisition opportunities or the happenstance of ambitious and vigorous political leadership can lead to the expansion of the open space activities of some government units into areas considered the logical province of other levels. Nevertheless, a second model, the *interventionist model*, has grown up within this tradition. In this model a higher level of government has, in addition to its open space responsibility assigned by the hierarchical model, a direct obligation to provide user-oriented open spaces when a lower level of government cannot do so.

This notion of latent responsibility that is the basis of the interventionist model is not uniquely characteristic of public open space; it is found in many areas of government concern. In open space as in other matters, this notion of responsibility has gained acceptance as the capacities of many local governments have been nearly overwhelmed by the explosive expansion of the suburbs and the fiscal decay of the center cities. It is not surprising then that many policies based on the interventionist norm of responsibility have been directed toward providing urban open spaces and justified by the limitations placed on local capacities by tight financial straits or political fragmentation. The National Park Service's Parks for People Program, involving the federal government in open space in metropolitan areas and leading to the establishment of Gateway National Park in the New York metropolitan area and Golden Gate National Park in the San Francisco region, has grown out of a federal assumption of interventionist responsibility. Discussing federal intervention in what had previously been considered the concerns of lower levels of government, Tannenbaum writes that "there is a real question whether the National Park Service and the Department of the Interior of which it is a part, would not now prefer to act directly, instead of indirectly through the states, in Metropolitan Area resource matters."[29]

This intervention has several lower level counterparts. Pennsylvania has acquired Point State Park in downtown Pittsburgh, and New Jersey has developed Liberty State Park in the urbanized northeastern part of the state. Again in New Jersey, the Essex County Park System has come to play a strong role in the direct provision of open space facilities to Newark, its major city. Newark's municipal park system, the smallest in acres per capita of the nation's large city park systems, has much of its responsibilities borne by the Essex County system, many units of which are within or just outside the municipal boundaries and therefore serve as de facto city parks.

Generally, such intervention is welcomed by the lower level governments. Many would agree with Heckscher that, as a general rule, the higher the level of government, the better the management and administration. Some warnings have been raised, nevertheless, usually stressing the theme that the more remote the government unit, the less sensitive to unique needs it is likely to be. Dunn made this point in an argument against direct federal involvement in the open space problems of the cities. Little warned that problems of remoteness and insensitivity were inherent in increased state involvement in small-scale open space preservation in exurban areas.[30]

Taken together, these practical traditions, normative models, and caveats leave unclear the degree to which open space clients and open space functions are to be exclusively assigned to particular levels of government or shared among many. One thing that is clear, however, is that the presence of these distinct traditions and their concomitant models of responsibility have introduced a great deal of latitude for role definition and policy making at all levels of government. It is for the states that the ambiguity associated with this latitude is most pronounced, however.

The Problem of Choice for the States

The states, termed "the keystones of the American arch" by Elazar, occupy a position between the federal government above and the local governments below that gives them two surfaces of interaction. Because of this intermediate position, state decisions must be tightly meshed with related decisions at the federal and local level for many government functions.[31] Already mentioned has been the states' long interaction with the federal government in open space provision. They have been the beneficiaries of federal largesse in the form of advice and guidance on open space matters and occasionally outright grants of land and transfers of open space facilities.

Eventually the states were pressed to assume lower level open space responsibilities when the large-scale suburbanization of cities after World War II created two distinct problems that overwhelmed local governments. One was at the vanguard of suburban expansion; the other, in its wake. Willbern observes that "the growth in the use of the automobile and the freeway, along with accompanying changes in the location of industry, shops, offices, and homes have produced so great a change in the degree of urban growth as to constitute a fundamental change in kind."[32] This "fundamental change in kind" presented municipal governments with a new range of demands and problems well beyond past experience. On the edge of the metropolis the range of services demanded was fundamentally different from that traditionally provided in the central residential areas of the city.[33] Roads took on a new meaning, and new zoning and land use regulation had to be worked out from scratch. There was little in the accumulation of municipal tradition to guide the suburban municipality beyond the inadequate and usually inappropriate traditions of small town government. Furthermore, the new mobility created questions of governing responsibility that had not been raised before. Willbern viewed the states as having the ultimate responsibility for solving these problems, or at least for filling the vacuum with interim solutions while municipalities came to grips with the problem.[34]

The sheer size of fiscal responsibility that fell on the local governments on the suburban periphery was also an overwhelming problem. All the roads, schools, and recreational and other facilities required placed an enormous and sometimes unmanageable strain on municipal resources. When municipalities could not manage to finance all locally performed services, many people thought ultimate responsibility for them should fall on the state.[35] The combination of suburban mobility, the financial overload on municipalities, and the fragmentation of local governments made provision of public open space seem particularly to require state assumption of responsibility: "With the ever increasing mobility of people, there is an adequate basis for state financial assistance to all local units of government, as many recreational facilities benefit residents whether they reside within or outside the jurisdiction of the government that builds the facility."[36] According to Chapin, the fiscal and organizational stresses of suburbanization and the new demands for public service attending the suburban lifestyle had torn apart the old order of public open space provision. Any new order would involve an expanded role of the state on the metropolitan periphery.[37]

The second problem calling for the assumption of state responsibility occurred in the older, more central areas of the metropolis. There the suburban expansion was also creating massive problems for local government. Unable to expand their spatial jurisdiction as the functional city expanded outward, central cities found themselves with a decreasing fraction of metropolitan residents and a decreasing fraction of metropolitan economic activities under their jurisdiction.

Unfortunately, as the suburbs siphoned off the more economically favored urban residents, the remaining fraction of residents contained a
large percentage of those whose taxable incomes were low yet whose
demands for public services were high. Thus by the end of the 1950s,
the cities found themselves faced with a shrinking tax base and increasing service demands. Once again, the states seemed to many to
have the ultimate responsibility for problems created by the dynamics
of urban growth and change.[38] As the provision of urban open space
was one of a range of responsibilities the center-city governments
could no longer adequately discharge, it followed that it too fell to the
state.

In sum, the state's responsibilities for providing open space are by
no means clear or simple because it is heir to several role-defining traditions and theories. A state can narrowly and conservatively define
its role in accord with the hierarchical model; or it can define it expan-
sively, urban growth providing the rationale for its intervention both
on the suburban periphery and in the older, central districts. As we
shall see, this urban growth figured strongly in justifying New Jersey's Green Acres Program and prompted the crest of public interest
that brought the program into being.

3

The Origins of the Green Acres Program

Although the institution of the Green Acres Program in 1961 marked a sudden state commitment to an active policy of open space acquisition, there were important antecedents that prepared the way. In fact, the establishment of the Green Acres Program involved what Simon, Smithburg, and Thompson consider to be the typical stages of "prenatal" program development: recognition of a problem, advancement of proposals for its solution, legislative action on the proposals, and establishment of an agency.[1] Because of this, recounting the history of open space in New Jersey up to the establishment of the Green Acres Program is important for understanding subsequent open space policy. The main points of the sporadic interest in open space in the decades before the program show how the various traditions of open space provision came to be reflected in New Jersey's activities. The details of the immediate events leading to the program introduce those with a hand in the program's establishment and subsequent direction and reveal many aspects of the bureaucratic and political climate in which New Jersey's open space policy has evolved. Finally, the fact that, as Dunshire shows,[2] the way a program evolves may be strongly dependent on the administrative structure through which information and decisions flow, justifies an examination of the program's formal decision-making structure as initially established and subsequently modified.

Providing Public Open Space in New Jersey before the Green Acres Program

Early in the twentieth century, New Jersey, like so many states, established state departments of parks and forests after the national models and with federal encouragement. This hardly signaled a commitment to an aggressive policy of land acquisition, however, for acquisition usually depended on tax delinquency or fortuitous offerings. By World War II, the state forest system consisted largely of a scattering of infertile lands in the Pine Barrens of southern New Jersey and in the sparsely populated northwestern section of the state. Only two holdings, Lebanon State Forest and Stokes State Forest, were larger than 10,000 acres, and those two alone constituted two-thirds of the state forest holdings of 54,000 acres. The state park system's acreage was similarly concentrated; two-thirds of its acreage was located in Sussex County (see any map in this book for locations of counties), most of it consisting of undeveloped land adjacent to Stokes State Forest. State game lands, almost exclusively located in the Pine Barrens of Burlington and Ocean counties, added another 10,000 acres to state-owned open space.[3]

Also early in the twentieth century, New Jersey became a participant, albeit a rather reluctant one, with New York in the establishment of the Palisades Interstate Park Commission to acquire public open space along the Palisades of the Hudson River. Most of the commission's acquisitions, however, took place north of New Jersey's border in New York's Orange and Rockland counties, and the residents of New York City rather than of New Jersey were considered the primary beneficiaries of both the park lands provided and the scenic amenities preserved.[4]

While New Jersey was slowly accumulating public open space, its neighbors were moving more rapidly. By the late 1930s, the state's open space holdings ranked it well below its neighbors in per capita public open space (Table 1). Because acquisition awaited tax delinquency and private offerings, it is hard to speak of a conscious state open space policy beyond one of minimal commitment and passive opportunism. There was certainly no conscious commitment to one of the two acquisition models or traditions. The accumulated result of this minimal commitment was, however, a set of holdings in keeping with the hierarchical model, which assigned to the state responsibility for providing remote, resource-oriented open spaces. Urban land was expensive and not likely, to fall to government for nonpayment of taxes, and the same applied to suburban land. Also, the holders of urban property rarely had the sentimental attachment to it that frequently led rural landowners to offer the state land on the condition that it be preserved. Consequently the lands that did come to the state were undeveloped tracts, usually large, infertile and almost always remote from large centers of population. Furthermore, although sub-

Table 1. Recreational Facilities of Other States Compared with Those of New Jersey as of 1939

States	Estimated total population 1935	State reservations in acres				Acres per thousand inhabitants
		Parks	Forests	Other	Total	
Connecticut	1,673,000	11,565.0	66,424.0	238.0	78,227.0	46.8
Massachusetts	4,368,000	2,382.4	164,596.2	14,808.2	181,786.8	41.6
New York	13,219,000	140,773.2	2,345,600.0	41,239.7	2,527,612.9	191.2
Pennsylvania	9,890,000	31,064.0	1,630,000.0	12,491.7	1,673,555.7	169.2
New Jersey	4,281,000	18,004.0	54,338.0	9,960.0	82,302.0	19.2
California	6,287,000	289,317.9		3,854.3	293,172.2	46.6
Michigan	5,220,000	44,264.1	888,167.0	778.2	933,309.3	178.8

SOURCE: New Jersey State Planning Board, *Parks and Public Lands in New Jersey*, Trenton, 1941.
NOTE: California and Michigan both had large amounts of federal land within their borders by 1939. They had, nevertheless, much more state-owned land per capita than did New Jersey. Comparison of New Jersey with New York, with its vast Adirondack forest preserve, and with Pennsylvania, holding large amounts of land on the remote Allegheny Plateau, is probably somewhat specious. Comparisons with Massachusetts and Connecticut, states more similar to New Jersey in size and population density, are probably more useful.

urbanization had already transformed New Jersey's landscape by the beginning of the 1960s, it had not yet brought the inner cities to a point of financial crisis. Thus there was little pressure as yet to use open space as an instrument in dealing with the set of problems termed the urban crisis.

On the suburban periphery of American cities, where the fragmentation of local authority was most prevalent, the county rather than the state first stepped into the breach and became an important purveyor of public open space. The suburban counties of Cook and DuPage around Chicago and Westchester in New York built open space systems through the twenties and thirties, contemporary with their first flush of suburban development. The county forest preserve was the mainstay of the Illinois counties' open space systems. Counties around New York built parkways along rivers, established golf courses, set aside floodplains, and acquired natural sites of special interest. In New Jersey, Essex County took responsibility for providing public open space in the suburban tissue that formed to the north and west of Newark in the early twentieth century. As New York metropolitan expansion suburbanized much of northeastern New Jersey in the twenties and thirties, county park commissions were founded and took an active role in providing public open space in the newly suburbanizing areas. By the 1930s, Union County, which was like neighboring Essex County in its strong and active park commission, had developed one of the best county park systems in the nation.[5] In the meantime, the state was doing little to provide open space in metropolitan areas.

Although state open space activity was low key and disjointed before World War II, planning was ambitious, even though the political means of implementing the plans were not available. In 1934, the New Jersey State Planning Board was instituted, largely in response to federal prompting and largely subsidized by federal funds (which provided 80 percent of its operating expenses). It soon involved itself in open space planning. Although funding and prompting came from Washington, much of its planning philosophy and most of its prognostications came from the Regional Plan Association.

In 1928, the Regional Plan Association (RPA) published a detailed plan for the future of the metropolitan region.[6] Its basic assumption was that the existing infrastructure of the inner city precluded much planning there, whereas on the city's periphery there was still opportunity to channel urbanization into an orderly and balanced pattern. The RPA considered a balanced pattern to be one that included a system of open spaces in the form of local and regional parks placed with consideration for accessibility and suitability. For New Jersey the RPA's plan recommended quickly setting aside suitable places for recreation facilities to accommodate the future growth that new transportation links across the Hudson River were sure to bring.[7]

In New York, the Long Island State Park Commission, under the directorship of Robert Moses, ambitiously carried out many of the RPA's recommendations. Parkways connected the city to large regional parks on the metropolitan periphery. Beth Page and Sunken Meadow State Parks were established on Long Island, and Jones Beach was developed to national acclaim.[8] Such a program could not fail to affect New Jersey's open space plans.

The New Jersey State Planning Board's *Parks and Public Lands in New Jersey*, a plan issued in 1941, showed the twin influences of the Regional Plan Association and of Robert Moses. It was permeated with a sense of urgency, with a need to plan for the inevitable before it was too late: "The tempo of land development and land speculation is again on the upturn in many parts of the state. Some of the needed park sites will never be cheaper than they are now. Some, such as the better shore-park locations, are soon to be spoiled or disposed of in other ways."[9] The state's planning board, like the Regional Plan Association, advocated comprehensive open space planning: "A hit-or-miss procedure will get nowhere; there must be a plan showing what is needed, and where; and a stated policy, procedure, and program for gradually and opportunistically putting that plan into effect."[10] For Island Beach, a 2,000-acre, 10-mile-long section of the Atlantic barrier island that had remained the property of a preservation-minded family while the rest of the shore was being developed, the planners proposed enormous facilities modeled after those at Jones Beach. They recommended parkways following major water courses such as the Delaware River, and these too imitated New York's ambitious projects. Following the Regional Plan's suggestion and using Robert Moses's Long Island parks for models, New Jersey's planning board proposed a large park in the meadowlands of Bergen and Hudson counties, one that would act as a surrogate for the local open spaces the region's municipalities were unable to provide.

New Jersey's plan was not entirely modeled after New York precedents, however, nor did it follow completely the recommendations of the Regional Plan. It could not reasonably do so, for New Jersey's planning board had the entire state to consider, not just the northeastern metropolitan counties. It recommended putting much of the

Pine Barrens and the forested uplands of the northwestern region of
the state into public domain. Here its purpose was preserving public
planning options; public recreation was a secondary concern.

The planning board proposed the establishment of a bond fund to
finance the implementation of its recommendations. It further suggested that the recommended state program of acquiring, developing,
and maintaining open space be the responsibility of one consolidated
state agency. (An exception provided for separate administration of
fish and game and watershed land.) Neither suggestion came to fruition, and World War II put them out of consideration. In the years
immediately after the war, more land came into the state's park, game
land, and forest systems. But just as before the war, owner-initiated
offerings usually prompted state acquisitions. There was little comprehensive acquisition planning, and the cost of acquisitions was covered out of the state's general fund as the need arose.

In 1951, a state development plan appeared that incorporated many
of the suggestions and much of the spirit of the 1941 *Park and Public
Lands* plan.[11] It recommended rapid acquisition in the face of rising
prices and rapid conversion of land to urban use: "Of first importance
is acquisition of the needed lands. This is especially true for the areas
of exceptional recreational value such as some of the proposed sea-
shore park sites, some of the river-front properties, and lands close to
the metropolitan centers. Such areas are most subject to contrary
development and exploitation and they are day by day becoming
spoiled or prohibitively expensive. Once the land is assured, development can follow at a more leisurely pace."[12] Among the specific open
space recommendations carried over from the 1941 report were that
the meadowlands be developed as a metropolitan park; that scenic
land along the state's waterways be acquired, both for parks and parkways; and that Island Beach be acquired and developed as the pre-
mier public bathing area on the state's Atlantic coast. It recommended
that large tracts of the Pine Barrens be added to the state's holdings as
a forest preserve and managed in a manner similar to New York's
Adirondack Forest Preserve. It suggested that many of the rocky
ridge tops and much of the highlands of northwestern New Jersey be
brought into the public domain as park and forest. It also suggested a
bond issue to establish a fund for the purchase of such lands.

The publication of the 1951 plan received considerable favorable
publicity in the press, which urged the state government to follow the
plan's recommendations. Three years later, in 1954, Island Beach was
acquired by the state. In the same year, the Wharton Tract, the state's

largest private holding, was acquired and added to south Jersey's public forests. These two acquisitions and other, lesser state acquisitions of the 1950s were, nevertheless, financed out of the general fund. The state established neither an ongoing acquisition program nor the means of financing one.[13]

Before the initiation of the Green Acres Program, a disjointedness prevailed in state open space policy. As is all too common in public planning, there seemed to be a lack of connection between planning and policy.[14] The planners operated in what Needleman and Needleman termed the encapsulated mode, with study and recommendation forming the narrow boundaries of their authority.[15] Still, there was no lack of recommendations, most of which envisioned an ambitious role for the state whereby it would acquire large, regional open space in accordance with a long-range plan. They also advocated an interventionist role whereby the state would act quickly in the face of metropolitan expansion to buy land primarily of local use and benefit that municipalities could not themselves afford. It was also the state's responsibility, they argued, to provide compensating open space where urban municipalities found their opportunities foreclosed by overdevelopment. Yet actual open space acquisition proceeded disjointedly, uncoordinated from one land-holding unit to another, seemingly heedless of the accumulation of planning reports. "There were no real plans or priorities; someone wanted this piece, someone wanted another,"[16] is the way a state planning official remembers the period.

With scarce resources, the possibilities of serious, long-term planning were limited. Every dollar had to be stretched, and this was done by waiting for the good buys to come to the state. It precluded deciding what was wanted and going out to get it whatever the cost. Financing dependent on annual appropriations further inhibited long-range planning. The institution of the Green Acres Program with an ample, predictable source of funding changed everything. Realistic long-term planning; the routinization of acquisitions; and conscious, articulated state open space policy became possible.

Public Open Space Becomes a Public Issue

In the late 1950s, there was a surge of national interest in the preservation of open space in the face of what appeared to be its continuous and increasingly rapid conversion to other uses.[17] The surge was simi-

lar in its seeming spontaneity to the surge of interest in ecology a decade later, but there was no discrete focal event like Earth Day associated with it. Perhaps because of this, no such organized movement
formed, but the emerging sense of open space scarcity as a public
problem led to widespread notions of government responsibility for
its solution.[18]

One source sees the origins of the swelling interest in public open
space in the publicity surrounding the Echo Park controversy.[19] An alliance of conservation groups, which included the Sierra Club, the Is-
saak Walton League, and the National Parks and Recreation Association, fought to prevent the building of a dam across the Green River.
Preservationists confronted the apostles of efficient use. It was the
stuff of morality plays, and newspapers kept it in the public's eye for
weeks.[20] The controversy caught Congress by surprise. After it was
resolved (with a decision not to build the dam), but before it was forgotten, Congress, aroused by the dam's threat to the Dinosaur National Monument, appointed the Outdoor Recreation Resources Review Commission (ORRRC) and gave it three interrelated charges:

To determine the outdoor recreation wants and needs of the American people
now and what they will be in the years 1976 and 2000.

To determine the recreation resources of the Nation available to satisfy those
needs now and in the years 1976 and 2000.

To determine what policies and programs should be recommended to ensure
that the needs of the present and future are adequately and efficiently met.[21]

Laurence Rockefeller was appointed chairman, and under him a large
staff was assembled. The ORRRC study was launched with much
publicity. Interim reports routinely appeared, and press releases kept
the commission and its work before the public. Although the ORRRC
was initially concerned primarily with great western open spaces and
federal recreation responsibility, its base of concern was soon wid-
ened. It came to see a great need for local and state assumption of
responsibility for providing open space, especially in metropolitan
areas.

By the late 1950s, the RPA was predicting a doubling or a tripling
of the physical area of the metropolis within the next twenty-five
years.[22] Also during the time the ORRRC was active, Gottmann's idea
of a developing megalopolis—a vast, unplanned conurbation stretch-
ing from Boston to Washington—was gaining currency.[23] The ORRRC
study plus the predictions of accelerating metropolitan growth led to
a flurry of magazine and newspaper articles on the need to get much

more open space into the public domain. A point always stressed was a need to act quickly; to wait would mean the loss of many prime tracts to development. Furthermore, if the current escalation of land prices on the metropolitan periphery should continue, government would soon find itself without the resources to acquire sufficient open space. The Council of State Governments suggests that this surge of media attention caused country club members, farmers, land planners, hunters, bird watchers, and urban citizens who simply liked to get outdoors all to coalesce into a loose alliance of activists. Their aim was to force government to assume increased responsibility for acquiring open space.[24]

Government response to this crest of interest was not long in coming. On the federal level, Congress, prompted by the ORRRC, established the Land and Water Conservation Fund in 1961. The fund was to enable the federal government to provide matching grants to states and municipalities for their open space projects, which could include scenic, conservation, recreation, and development-containing objectives. The money could be used for both land acquisition and the construction of recreation facilities.

Much attention fell on the states, especially those with metropolitan areas within their borders, inspiring in them a great sense of responsibility for providing open space. The Council of State Governments said, "There is a clear recognition that states must act quickly and decisively to conserve open space in the face of rapid urban and suburban growth."[25] Chapin, referring to the states, said, perhaps not quite accurately but reflecting the spirit of the times, "For the first time government is awakening to the urgent need to preserve sufficient land in relatively undeveloped form."[26]

A number of states undertook studies that examined the need for expanded state open space acquisition. The title of the New York Department of Conservation report, *Now or Never*, nicely summarized both the mood of the reports and their common conclusion: the states had to act quickly.[27] In 1961, New York passed its Land Acquisition Bond Act calling for the establishment of a $100 million bond fund to be used for public open space acquisition.[28] Most of the money would be spent for the expansion of existing state parks, the establishment of new ones, and the increase of state game-land holdings. The balance of the fund would be used for matching grants-in-aid to counties and municipalities for their open space acquisitions.

Thus by 1961, public open space had become a vital issue of interest from the national to the municipal level. Responsibilities were being sorted out among various levels of government, with the states assuming a large share. They in turn were conducting studies, feeling their way into this new sense of responsibility, and beginning to act.[29]

The Program Is Proposed

In spite of the rising general interest in open space preservation, before September 1960, it had not yet become a major public issue in New Jersey.[30] In that month, however, the RPA, long a respected if not always an effective voice in policy formation in the metropolitan region, issued a report that made it a major issue.

Largely in response to the formation of the ORRRC and the consequent rise of regional interest in open space, the RPA, in association with the Metropolitan Regional Council (an unofficial body made up of the county executives of the metropolitan region), undertook a survey of the New York metropolitan area's open space needs. Like the ORRRC study, the RPA's Park, Recreation and Open Space Project was a major undertaking; and in 1960, its reports appeared in four volumes. The title of the final summarizing report of the project, *The Race for Open Space*, implied the most important conclusion of the study: that the metropolitan governments were in a race with the private economic forces of metropolitan expansion for scarce open land, much of which should remain as open space for the public good.

When *The Race for Open Space* was released in September 1960, newspapers, radio, and television gave its findings and recommendations extensive coverage; and the findings put New Jersey on the spot.[31] In recreational open space, RPA data showed that, among the states of the metropolitan region, New Jersey had the greatest gap between that actually available and the estimated amount needed. In a detailed data presentation of recreational needs, the RPA matched county, local, and state holdings against projected demand in 1985. The data made stark points. On a local level, New Jersey's section of the metropolitan region averaged .3 acres of small municipal park per 1,000 inhabitants, less than half of the minimum of 1 acre per 1,000 inhabitants proposed by the National Park and Recreation Association and accepted as the minimum adequate amount by the RPA. In larger municipal parks, New Jersey had .4 acres per 1,000 of population against minimum standards of 5 per 1,000. The nine New Jersey counties within the region had, among them, 16,525 acres of county park land, against a projected 1985 demand for 110,000 acres. As for state open space, the report broke down acquisitions by period of purchase and showed that, after great acreage acquisitions in the first half of the 1950s, there was an absolute hiatus in land acquisition in the late fifties. (In fact, a single purchase, the 1954 acquisition of the Wharton Tract, accounted for the bulk of New Jersey's acquired acreage in the first half of the 1950s.)

The report urged New Jersey to act immediately. It suggested that New Jersey establish a bond-financed fund for open space acquisition, using New York State's recently established bond fund as a model. It urged state emphasis on land acquisition; development of facilities on the land could follow at a more leisurely pace, it argued. The report also recommended that the state take an active role in insuring that local governments met their open space responsibilities. To this end, it suggested that some of the funds from the bond issue be assigned to a local assistance program. Finally, it recommended long-term, comprehensive open space planning.

Although the report, with its implicit criticism of the state's past efforts to acquire adequate open space, was the cause of some embarrassment within the state government, the state's Department of Conservation and Economic Development (the department responsible for the state's public open space) received it enthusiastically.[32] Throughout the late 1950s, those responsible for the provision and preservation of open space felt hamstrung by what they saw as a level of funding woefully inadequate for the proper discharge of their responsibilities. The Division of Fish, Game, and Shellfisheries saw the decline in state agriculture and the shift from grain to truck farming as deleterious to the game wildlife habitat.[33] These conditions, according to the division, increased the importance of publicly owned and managed wildlife areas. It wanted a threefold increase in state game land to compensate for shifting agricultural conditions. The Division of Parks and Forestry considered the immediate popularity of Island Beach State Park and the Wharton Tract (renamed the Wharton State Forest when the state acquired it) when they were opened to the public indicative of a vast unmet demand for state parks and recreational facilities. The Bureau of State and Regional Planning looked at the state's population growth figures and the land price increases for the previous decade and urged the acquisition of open space while there was still time and money available to integrate public open space facilities into areas of private development.[34]

These three units, plus the Division of Water Resources, had been meeting regularly since 1955 on the department's Land Use Committee. On it they discussed their problems, and through it they issued reports arguing for expanded funding and an aggressive program of open space acquisition. The reports had little impact on a fiscally conservative legislature and a disinterested governor (Robert Meyner). Then, with the swelling interest in public open space in the late 1950s, the division heads in the Department of Conservation and Economic Development suggested to Commissioner Bontempo that the time was right to try to persuade the administration to increase open space funding levels. In a memo dating from early in 1960, the head of the Division of Fish, Game, and Shellfisheries suggested to the department commissioner that perhaps he could capitalize on the publicity surrounding the passage of New York's open space bill. The commissioner bided his time. Then in September of that year, with the release of *The Race for Open Space*, the commissioner felt the time was right to propose to the governor the establishment of a long-term acquisition plan. He was correct; Governor Meyner had been aware of the crest of concern for public open space. The governor responded favorably to the commissioner's arguments and asked for a report detailing the need for such a plan in New Jersey. The commissioner in turn asked his department's Land Use Committee to prepare one.

The Land Use Committee worked quickly. Two months after the appearance of *The Race for Open Space*, the New Jersey study's findings and recommendations appeared in a report, largely the work of the Division of State and Regional Planning, entitled *The Need for a State Recreation Land Acquisition and Development Program*.[35] It accepted the RPA's estimates of future needs and incorporated them into its final report. In fact, it arrived at statewide open space demand figures by simply extrapolating from the RPA's demand estimates for New Jersey's nine metropolitan counties. The report repeated the RPA's assertion that recreation had become an indispensable part of American life. It presented projections of exponentially increasing population, income, and mobility and coupled them with a projected decrease in the length of the work week to justify estimates of rapidly increasing demand for open space for recreational pursuits of all kinds. It repeated the RPA's suggestion for a grant-in-aid program for lower levels of government. Because New Jersey had a Division of Local Government providing assistance to towns on budget and debt matters, such a recommendation could be considered a natural extension of current state interest in local problems. The report recommended that an ongoing program of state acquisition be coordinated among the divisions represented on the Land Use Committee. Perhaps because it was widely known that the governor did not favor bond issues, the report refrained from suggesting a means of financing such a program.

The Commissioner of Conservation and Economic Development reviewed the plan, approved it, and sent it on to the governor with a covering memo suggesting that a general obligation bond issue be floated to create an acquisition fund for the program. After hearing further arguments from the commissioner, the governor approved the idea of the land acquisition program, now named the Green Acres Program.[36] He went against his general opposition to bond financing on principle and agreed to finance it through a bond issue. Enabling legislation for the Green Acres bond issue was incorporated into his legislative program for the following year, and the details of the program's organization were worked out by the Land Use Committee in consultation with the governor's staff.

A figure of $60 million was settled on for the bond issue. For New Jersey, given its tradition of extreme parsimony in state government, it was a lot of money. Of that amount, $40 million would be used to acquire land the state itself would own and manage through the Division of Fish, Game, and Shellfisheries and the Division of Parks and Forestry. The balance, $20 million, would be used to establish a matching fund to make grants to local governments to aid them in acquiring open spaces that they would own and manage. According to the plan, a local government would put up 50 percent of a tract's purchase price, and the state would provide the remainder with a grant from the fund. The program would be for acquisition only; there was some discussion of earmarking some of the fund for development, but this was ruled out for both planning and political reasons. First, any diversion from acquisition seemed unwise in light of the perceived need to acquire land ahead of private developers. Once the land was safely in public hands, development plans could be undertaken at a more leisurely pace. Second, many state officials thought any such diversion of funds from acquisition might lessen the bond referendum's appeal to the voters.[37] Once drawn up, the bill to put the bond referendum before the voters was speedily brought to the floor of both houses and passed unanimously.

Selling the Program

With the Green Acres bond question scheduled to go on the ballot in November, the Land Use Committee prepared to promote it with a high-powered, two-step campaign. The first step was to convince the state's organized interest groups of the plan's merits. Then, with their active help, the program could be sold to the voting public through a mass-media campaign. It seemed like a good strategy; groups like the state's Chamber of Commerce, the AFL-CIO, and the teacher's union were politically active and wielded powerful influence in the state. Unfortunately, although these groups had no objections to the Green Acres Program and indeed approved of it, they were not very interested in it. Open space preservation simply was not a salient issue for them, and they were not willing to promote it actively. The Land Use Committee would have to display what Downs called spontaneous entrepreneurship and take the initiative in promoting the program if it were to be successful.[38]

It set up the Bonds "Yes" Committee and stocked it with leading citizens, primarily board chairmen and retired politicians. From the beginning, the Bonds "Yes" Committee was an instrument of state administrators within the various divisions that sat on the Land Use Committee. The degree to which this was the case is evidenced by the fact that an employee of the Land Use Committee's parent department (Conservation and Economic Development) was appointed as the Bonds "Yes" Committee's executive director, and he later became the Green Acres program administrator.

Although unwilling to take the initiative, the state's organized interests were willing to lend support to the campaign once it was underway. Perhaps at another time the program would have been considered a land grab or a further encroachment of government into areas outside its proper domain, but in 1961, it was widely viewed as a legitimate state undertaking. Although an increased tempo of state open space acquisition had little direct bearing on the more immediate goals of the state's business, labor, or professional groups, supporting it put them in step with what was clearly prevailing sentiment.[39] Also, they might have reasoned that, in the absence of any compelling reasons to the contrary, why not oblige a government unit that wanted support? The favor might be returned some day. Although most of the state's major interest groups had little to gain from the Green Acres Program, the cost of supporting it was minimal.

Eventually, almost all the state's major organized interest groups went on record in favor of it. There were only two exceptions. The New Jersey Taxpayers Association, a group that advocated conservative fiscal policy, had no objection to the goals of the program but opposed bond financing on principle. In a press release, the association said it would have supported the program had it been set up with financing out of annual legislative appropriations. The League of Women Voters, thinking there was insufficient time to study the issue as thoroughly as necessary, took no stand on the bond referendum.[40]

With the state's interest groups lined up in support, the program's active backers—state planners, foresters, park administrators, and game management personnel—sold Green Acres to the public through the Bonds "Yes" Committee. The campaign was skillfully run. The committee distributed eye-catching bumper stickers and professionally prepared information kits with brochures and fact sheets. It bought radio spots and issued frequent press releases. The tone of the campaign was dramatic and emotional; promotional flyers had "before" scenes of verdant dales and "after" scenes of row after row of new, raw subdivision housing.[41] The overall tone of the campaign was unabashedly preservationist. It worked by touching deep and perhaps inchoate public fears through symbol manipulation.

The campaign made frequent use of the bulldozer image. Its sound was used as a backdrop to dialogue in the campaign's radio advertisements. In brochures a bulldozer blade was pictured coming squarely at the viewer, with a couple of unearthed trees on its blade. The imagery was powerful. By implying that they would stay the bulldozer and the forces it represented, the program's sponsors were selling more than a bond issue; they were offering a symbolic antidote to a much broader malaise. Willbern saw state governments of this period as floundering in their efforts to meet suburban aspirations for the good life.[42] Here was a program whose symbolic appeal went directly to the deepest suburbanite aspirations and fears. It offered to preserve the good life from the metropolitan expansion that threatened to destroy it.

On Election Day 1961, the bond issue was approved by a substantial majority of the voters, and the Green Acres Program has been in operation at the center of the state's open space preservation efforts ever since. A second bond issue, for $80 million, was approved by the voters in 1971; and a third, for $200 million, was approved in 1974, a year that saw all other bond referenda soundly defeated at the polls. Most recently, another $200 million bond issue to finance the program well into the 1980s was approved in 1978.[43]

With the approval of the first bond issue in 1961, New Jersey followed the precedent set by New York the previous year, when its voters had approved a similar bond issue establishing a major, long-term program of open space acquisition. The following four years saw eight other states follow their lead, and by 1977 twenty-three states had established such programs.

Program Structure

On approval of the Green Acres referendum the Department of Conservation and Economic Development (DCED) quickly established the administrative organization necessary to run an ongoing program of open space acquisition. The decision-making machinery contained both entirely new administrative units and preexisting units given new responsibilities in connection with the program. This assignment of new responsibility to existing departments already active in the provision of open space is consistent with the observation of March and Simon that "as new situations arise, the construction of an entirely new program from detailed elements is rarely contemplated."[44] Rather, existing elements are used as much as possible. There were three focuses of responsibility, the land-holding units, the Land Use Committee, and the Green Acres administrative offices, each with separate, if not entirely defined, roles in running the program.

For many decades before Green Acres, the DCED's land-holding units—the Division of Parks and Forestry and the Division of Fish, Game, and Shellfisheries—were the government units upon which fell most of the responsibilities for administering the state's public open space. The advent of Green Acres did nothing to change their fundamental roles or responsibilities; they continued to administer the state's parks, forests, and game land and to make their own plans. They still received offerings and evaluated them against their own internally formulated criteria. Whereas before, they had requested acquisition funds through legislative appropriations for tracts they wished to purchase, they now, however, applied for Green Acres grants through the Land Use Committee.

The second administrative component in the operation of the program was the DCED's Land Use Committee. The committee, like the land-holding units themselves, long antedated the Green Acres Program. Made up of representatives of various divisions within the DCED, it had been established in 1955 to advise the department commissioner on land use policy, although in the fifties it had little real scope and met infrequently. The establishment of the Green Acres Program brought it considerable formal power in determining state open space policy. First, it was given responsibility for setting the broad policy goals of the program. Second, it was to receive grant requests from the land-holding units and evaluate them for appropriateness and conformity with these broad goals. These two charges added up to a central formal role in shaping and implementing open space policy. A grant request approved by the committee then went to the commissioner, who had final say in any acquisition made with Green Acres funds.

All those DCED units with an interest in public open space were represented on the committee, and this naturally included the land-holding units.[45] But it also included the Division of State and Regional Planning, the source of most state-level planning activity. The division viewed its job on the committee as insuring that open space policy evolved in accordance with what it deemed sound and equitable planning principles.[46] Recently elevated in status from the lower level "bureau" designation, the division had long been especially concerned with unregulated metropolitan expansion and its attendant effects on land use throughout the state. Consequently, it was a strong supporter of the Green Acres Program. Until the program was established, it had little opportunity to do more than draw up open space plans and issue reports to a limited readership. Now, through its membership on the Land Use Committee, it would have the opportunity to do more.

When the program was established, the post of Green Acres program administrator was created within the DCED. The program administrator was responsible for the third component of the Green Acres administrative structure, the unit that dealt with the mundane matters of running the program on a day-to-day basis and with coordinating state open space activities with both federal and local ones. This unit, officially titled the Office of Legal Services and Real Estate, was commonly referred to as the "Green Acres office"; and although it did have other responsibilities, servicing the Green Acres Program was its most important role.

The Green Acres office had two sections. The first, the land acquisition unit, was responsible for acquiring properties for the state under the program. It handled all acquisitions made by the DCED, whether financed by Green Acres funds or not. Almost all of these acquisitions were made under the Green Acres Program, however, leading to its common-parlance label, "the state Green Acres office." This unit was responsible for contact with the owners of properties to be acquired, title searches and clearances, surveys, negotiation, condemnation litigation, appraisals, and most of the technical work that accompanies state acquisition of private property. Although the state Green Acres office had no formal responsibility for setting policy, its estimates of the amount of work involved and the difficulties to be encountered in acquiring a tract were taken into account during consideration of proposed acquisitions.

The second unit of the Green Acres office was the local acquisition section. This unit was responsible for the administration of the local matching fund; it disseminated information about the local program, advised local governments about application procedures, and processed their applications. The local acquisition section, like the state acquisition unit, was largely responsible for providing technical and clerical services needed to run the program; it was not formally involved in policy making.

Above these three administrative components was the DCED commissioner, who had a great deal of discretionary power over program as final decision maker on all grants made from the fund. The commissioner could reject a grant request simply because he thought it was "not in keeping with the goals of the program,"[47] knowing that any court challenge to his decision would have to overcome the presumption of administrative competence. The commissioner was also the conduit of political demands into the program because of his position as a member of the governor's cabinet, which brought him into frequent contact with local politicians and members of the state legislature.

Over the years this administrative arrangement has remained relatively unchanged. The three-part decision structure has persisted in spite of government reorganizations that have shifted departmental responsibilities for the program. In the first of these reorganizations, in 1967, the Division of State and Regional Planning was moved out of the DCED and into the newly formed Department of Community Affairs. This put organizational distance between it and the other important members of the Land Use Committee. The consequences of this distance are discussed below. Then in 1970, another reorganization of the state government disbanded the Green Acres parent department, the DCED, and established a new Department of Environmental Protection (DEP). Overall responsibility for the program was shifted to the newly created DEP, as were the Green Acres office and the landholding units. Figure 1 shows how responsibilities for the Green Acres Program are allocated within the DEP. The Division of State and Regional Planning was unaffected by this reorganization; it remained where it was in the Department of Community Affairs.

The Office of Environmental Review, a new office created with the inception of the DEP, came to play a role in the Green Acres Program. To it was assigned responsibility for liaison with the federal government, which, with the establishment of its Bureau of Outdoor Recreation (BOR) and several open space grant-in-aid programs in the early 1960s, had become increasingly committed to an interventionist position. In keeping with this liaison role, the Office of Environmental

Review was charged with the preparation of the state's comprehensive recreation plan. Although the overt purpose of the plan is to guide recreation planning in the state, its compilation by the state (and its approval by the BOR in Washington) is a precondition of state eligibility for federal grants from the BOR-administered Land and Water Conservation Fund (LWCF).

Under the provisions of the LWCF Act, grant money is apportioned out to the states according to a formula based on population. Once apportioned to the states, they themselves decide how their share will be distributed to lower levels of government. In New Jersey the Office of Environmental Review has this responsibility. Although this does not directly involve it in the dispersal of Green Acres funds, the office often works closely with the Green Acres local grant section to assemble a grant package that covers almost the entire cost of a local acquisition, with 50 percent from Green Acres and the balance from the LWCF.[48]

With the formation of the DEP, the Commissioner's Advisory Committee on Open Lands Conservation was established. It is the successor to the disbanded DCED's Land Use Committee, and its role in the Green Acres Program is similar: "Consonant with DEP's role in planning and implementing an open space land acquisition program, the Advisory Committee shall make recommendations and advise the Commissioner on matters of acquisition policy, projects and programming."[49] Its membership includes the land-holding units and the offices within the DEP with responsibilities toward the Green Acres Program, namely the Office of Environmental Review and the Office of Legal Services and Real Estate. It also includes representatives of units outside the DEP with an occasional or peripheral interest in open space policy, the Department of Agriculture and the Department of Transportation being perhaps foremost among them. These outside representatives on the committee are there largely to protect the interests of their departments and to insure a smooth meshing between the Green Acres Program and the activities of their units. For example, the Department of Transportation on occasion has alerted the committee to what it saw as potential conflict between Green Acres acquisition plans and the Department of Transportation's road-building plans. The Department of Agriculture is perpetually concerned with state activities that may have an adverse effect on agriculture and has occasionally protested the acquisition of land it believed would be more beneficial to the state under crops. As with the committee it replaced, the Commissioner's Advisory Committee is formally the policy center of the program.[50]

Figure 1. Organizational Chart for the Green Acres Program, Department

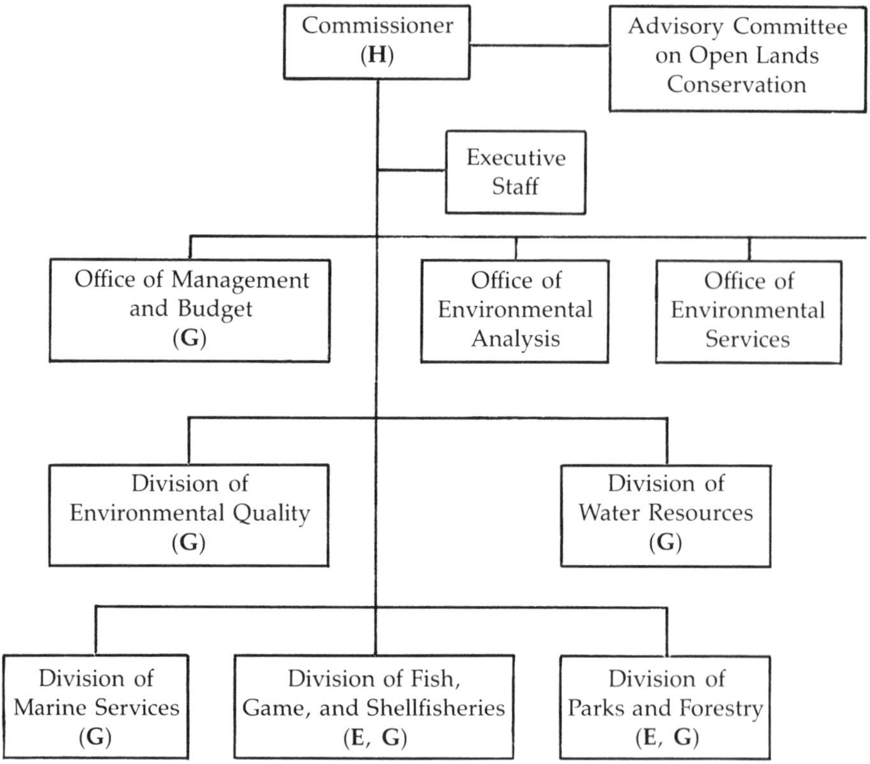

Nature of Involvement with Green Acres

A   Green Acres land acquisition and support services
B   Green Acres local assistance grants
C   Federal grants administration (land acquisition)
D   Open space and recreation planning
E   Operation of Green Acres acquisitions
F   Legal services and representation
G   Representation on Advisory Committee on Open Lands Conservation
H   Overall policy coordination
I   Legislative fiscal oversight (transfers and appropriations)

Source: New Jersey State Legislature, Office of Fiscal Affairs, *The New Jersey Green Acres Land Acquisition Program*, Division of Program Analysis Report, No. 6, Trenton, 1975, p. 6.

of Environmental Protection

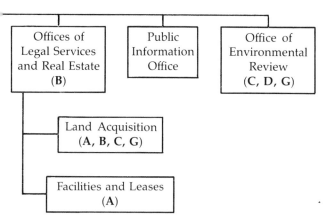

Other Agencies

| Department of Community Affairs, Division of State and Regional Planning (**D, G**) | Department of Law and Public Safety, Division of Law (Deputy Attorney General) (**F**) |
| N.J. State Legislature "Watchdog" Committee (**I**) | Department of Agriculture (**G**) |

In 1974, the uses to which Green Acres money could be put were extended to include the development (although not the maintenance) of public open spaces. Because the money from the first two bond issues could be used only for acquisition, the land-holding units and the local governments had used it to acquire properties that in some cases they could not afford to develop. Thus, a sizeable backlog of open space development projects eventually accumulated both at state and local levels. After 1974, Green Acres funds could be used to purchase recreational equipment, build access roads, and upgrade existing facilities, and the Green Acres administrative structure was modified accordingly. Both state and local sections now have subunits to handle the administration of development grants, which are dealt with similarly to acquisition grants. Smaller staffs are needed to handle development grants, however, for there is no negotiating with land owners, nor are there title searches or other time-consuming acquisition-related activities involved. Moreover, the grant applicants, whether local governments or units of the state government, do the engineering, architectural, and other work involved in preparing development grant requests; and this further reduces the time it takes the Green Acres office to process them.

In the mid and late 1970s, rising interest in the preservation of the Pine Barrens on southern New Jersey's outer coastal plain led to a spate of state government activity to this end, including the creation of the Office of Pineland Acquisitions within the DEP. The primary assignment of this office is to review proposals (from within or without state government) for public acquisitions within the Pine Barrens and establish a priority list for those it deems worthwhile. If a property on the list is given final approval by the commissioner, the acquisition is financed out of the Green Acres bond fund, while the Office of Real Estate and Legal Services handles the details of the acquisition much as it would handle any direct state Green Acres purchase.

In spite of the changes that have taken place, continuity rather than change predominates in the basic machinery of the decision making and in the focuses of formal power. The basic roles of the land-holding units have remained constant, as have the role of the local grants office and that of the state acquisition office. A Green Acres program administrator has always supervised the activities of both; a departmental coordinating committee has always been extant, if not active; and a department commissioner has always borne ultimate administrative responsibility for the decisions made under him.

It is evident that neither the structure of the Green Acres Program nor its formal allocation of decision-making authority offer much structural predisposition toward serving some interests to the neglect of others. Nor does structure provide many clues to how actual decision making will take place. For example, although the local grants program perforce involves the state in local open space matters, the state can choose to adopt a detailed, guiding policy or it can play a passive role, dispersing money as requested. The decision structure in the state program gives leeway to the land-holding units, each with its distinct clientele and its traditions of independent operation, and each of which has accumulated a set of holdings in keeping with the hierarchical model. The structure also assigns a strong formal role to the Division of State and Regional Planning, heir to a set of problems different from those of the land-holding units and long a spokesman for coordinated state open space policy. Furthermore, the steering committee—first the Land Use Committee of the DCED and now the DEP's Commissioner's Advisory Committee on Open Lands Conservation—has an explicit coordinating role. This may mean it will be little more than the sum of the interests of its constituent units, or it may mean it will have an independent, policy-influencing life of its own. Finally, there is the commissioner, first of the DCED, now of the DEP. Because of his great discretionary powers over the program, he can, at least in theory, mold it to his liking. All the potentially divergent interests and points of view that the formal decision-making structure admits into the policy arena make it necessary to look beyond mere structure, to examine the dynamics and politics of the program in each decision arena, to understand New Jersey open space policy.

4

State Acquisition Policy

The Green Acres Program involves the state in the provision of public open space on the one hand through direct state acquisition of open lands and on the other through grants made to local governments from the local matching fund. Although both activities are handled by Green Acres personnel and ultimate responsibility for both activities rests with the DEP commissioner, de facto decision making falls to different actors in the two sections of the program. Moreover, different criteria shape the decisions, policies, and results in each part of the program. It is thus best to examine separately first the state acquisitions and then, in the next chapter, the distribution of grants-in-aid from the local matching fund.

The Predispositions of Parks and Forestry

The primary responsibility of New Jersey's DEP Division of Parks and Forestry (hereafter, Parks and Forestry) is the administration of the state's forests and parks. Although in theory the park and forest systems have distinct missions and are each under a separate bureau within the division, the increasing demands for recreation in this most urbanized of states contributed to an early merging of roles. Initially parks were intensive recreation areas associated with sites of special natural or cultural value. High Point State Park, containing, as its name implies, the highest point in New Jersey, and Ringwood Manor State Park, containing a restored colonial iron-making complex, are examples. Forests were more extensive tracts, usually heavily wooded and suitable for timber harvesting. The recreational role of the forests soon emerged, however, with the Bureau of Forests continually expanding the number of campsites and recreation facilities on its holdings. Although management for conservation is still practiced in the state forests, timber harvesting has become progressively less important. Parks and Forestry is also the state's principal custodian of historic places. It manages such diverse historic sites as the site of Washington's crossing of the Delaware and the Proprietary House, the seat of New Jersey's government during the colonial period.

Before the Green Acres Program, Parks and Forestry had little choice in open space acquisitions beyond refusing what was offered. Because of low budgets and a lack of predictable purchase funds, it for the most part acquired fortuitous offerings and land fallen to the state for nonpayment of taxes. A division official said of acquisition policy, "Before the Green Acres Program we took what we could get."[1] The Green Acres Program changed all that: A large purchase fund was now available. Passive opportunism no longer had to be the division's modus operandi; it could begin to choose among policies and goals. The division has opted continually for the hierarchical model of narrowly defined state responsibility and has shaped acquisition policy accordingly. It has rejected the expansive, interventionist model whenever it has been suggested.

There are several reasons for this adherence to the hierarchical model and reluctance to deviate from it. First, the Green Acres Program was sold to the public, at least on a symbolic level, as an anti-development program; it was to save land from the bulldozer. Occasionally the program is taken to task by the media or by legislators for not "saving" as much land as originally hoped, and Parks and Forestry's use of Green Acres money comes in for evaluation on this land-saving criterion.[2] Second, although there is no direct correlation between number of acres acquired by Parks and Forestry and popular or official favor, in the absence of contravening circumstances, many acres look better than few. Third, low costs per acre are less likely to raise questions of extravagance and misuse of funds than are high costs per acre, regardless of the ultimate worth of the acquisition. An annual report showing large acquisitions at low per-acre costs looks good. Money spent in urban areas, or even in areas where land speculation has driven up prices, does not go far and does not produce large acquisitions. Liberty Park, 590 acres on the Jersey City waterfront, cost over $14 million, whereas the nearly 6,000-acre Wawayanda Tract in rural northwestern New Jersey cost only $1.8 million. The Liberty Park acquisition was subjected to legislative criticism for excessive money and opportunity costs; the acquisition of Wawayanda Tract was widely considered a great coup. The hierarchical model, with its logical association of state responsibility with large resource-oriented tracts, allows Parks and Forestry to seek out the best per-acre buys in scenic, rural areas with little regard for accessibility to large population clusters, which would inevitably drive up the cost of the land. At the same time, a policy aimed at acquiring these large, rural tracts allows the department to emphasize conservation as well as recreational goals.

Still another advantage of the hierarchical model to Parks and Forestry is that concentrating on rural holdings permits concentrating on servicing a select clientele: the motorized middle class, whose private means of transportation and habits of mobility give them easy access to open space, wherever in the state it may be. Concentrating on this middle-class clientele makes sense for Parks and Forestry administrators for two reasons. First, this group encompasses most of the social loci of political power, those excluded being mostly politically impotent and not likely to present effective demands for service. Second, those who arrive in parks in private autos are mostly families, and this works to mitigate supervisory and maintenance problems. Children enter the parks under the watchful eyes of parents, relatives, or parent surrogates; so their park behavior is structured by adult, largely middle-class norms. Difficulty of access to parks other than by automobile tends to filter out unsupervised youths.

In contrast, the interventionist mode, which makes the state responsible for providing local, intensive open space when lower levels of government cannot do so, offers several clear disadvantages to the state agency that must buy and administer such places. First, public open space in urban or suburban areas is expensive; land is dear, and development costs are high. The expensive, low-acreage acquisitions an interventionist policy entails would expose the state agency to charges of profligate spending. Economy has long been a watchword in the New Jersey legislature, and the DEP has always thought it necessary to listen carefully for stirrings of discontent over land costs.[3]

A second practical problem with the interventionist model, especially as applied in urban areas, grows out of a series of correlative relationships between neighborhood characteristics and land values. In residential areas there is usually an inverse relationship between population density and income. There is also a direct relationship between the mean income of an area and the rate at which land values are rising. Finally, there is another direct relationship between mean income and increase in population. Table 2 indicates the nature and strength of these relationships in New Jersey. Most of the state's major cities have low per-capita incomes, in many cases, still below $4,000 per year as of 1975. They also have high overall densities, frequently above ten thousand inhabitants per square mile. In these urban places, land values rise slowly, if at all; and population declines are more the rule than the exception. Putting parks in the poorest neighborhoods, especially in the absence of a coordinated program of neighborhood maintenance or redevelopment, is sure to draw criticism that the open space facilities being provided will have diminishing use and consequently diminishing social value as densities continue to decrease. Moreover, land in such areas often retains a high market value, making such a policy very expensive when measured in acres of open space provided.[4]

A third problem associated with such an interventionist policy arises over the size of the open spaces to be provided in urban areas. If land is acquired in small, scattered pieces, the appearance of the open space, and its uses as well, will in all likelihood be little different from that of a miscellaneous collection of lots rendered vacant by the random demolition of condemned buildings. On the other hand, if large pieces are acquired, expensive and unpopular condemnation is involved, which might further depopulate the area. Queale and Lynch, discussing the problems inherent in such a strategy in New Jersey, suggest that "open land or recreation use which requires the uprooting of large numbers of people would seem to be in conflict with the stated purposes of the urban state parks concept of bringing the park areas to where the people live."[5]

Fourth, an urban interventionist course would also expose Parks and Forestry to many of the social pathologies that considerably increase the cost of public services in urban areas. For example, contractors bidding on jobs in the state's larger cities routinely add 20 percent to their bids to cover the costs of complying with affirmative action regulations and of added security precautions.[6] Also, amateur and professional vandals have created the need for a new and expensive kind of preventive urban architecture that Parks and Forestry would rather avoid. Because administrative efficiency is often interpreted as securing the greatest material output for the dollar, state park officials would not like to be asked to justify the outlay of the going price (as of 1977) of $60,000 for a vandal-proof comfort station in an urban park in Newark. Parks and Forestry would much rather have the city of Newark buy such facilities itself, even if the state must give the city the money in the first place through the local program. In fact, when the whole matter of the limits of state respon-

Table 2. A Comparison of Selected New Jersey Municipalities for Various Characteristics in 1972

Municipality	Estimated mean income per capita 1975	Estimated population 1975	Estimated density per square mile 1975	Percentage land-value change 1962–1972	Estimated percentage change in population 1962–1975
		URBAN			
Hoboken	3,832	41,958	32,275	−11	−6
Trenton	4,164	100,027	13,337	2	−8
Newark	3,586	342,502	13,465	3	−10
Atlantic City	3,952	44,462	3,736	5	−23
Camden	3,478	92,585	10,666	7	−15
New Brunswick	4,696	45,012	8,184	38	6
Irvington	5,271	57,613	20,576	41	−2
Perth Amboy	4,542	36,833	8,095	49	0
Jersey City	4,555	242,143	16,528	63	−8
Elizabeth	5,028	105,744	9,045	80	2

Middletown	5,771	58,103	1,414	124	41
Princeton township	11,699	14,209	874	225	35
Chester township	6,552	4,552	157	246	111
East Brunswick	6,203	38,051	1,714	263	130
Paramus	6,575	28,124	2,717	307	21
North Caldwell	9,774	6,974	2,404	312	58
Hillsborough	5,735	13,885	253	334	51
Holmdel	6,629	7,517	420	347	150
Montvale	7,218	7,340	1,835	408	98
Franklin township[a]	5,758	31,091	663	455	55

SOURCES: New Jersey Department of Community Affairs, Division of State and Regional Planning, *New Jersey Municipal Profiles: Intensity of Urbanization*, Trenton, 1972; New Jersey Department of Labor and Industry, Division of Planning and Research, *Population Estimates for New Jersey*, Trenton, 1978; and U.S. Department of Commerce, Bureau of the Census, *Per Capita Money Income for New Jersey*, mimeograph, Washington, D.C., February, 1979.
[a]Somerset County.

sibility for providing open space was raised during the initial formulation of the Green Acres Program, Parks and Forestry strongly
supported the idea of a local matching fund. If the state aided municipal open space programs through such a grant program, state agencies with open space responsibilities could avoid being drawn into
the unsettled waters of direct service to the state's municipalities and,
above all, to its large cities.[7]

A fifth drawback of interventionist policy to a land-administering
agency grows out of the peculiarities of New Jersey politics. County-
level politics has always been important in the state. Historically, the
Democratic machines of the older urbanized counties and the en-
trenched suburban Republicans organization have wielded an inordi-
nate amount of power—to the disadvantage of the state government,
which was often seen as little more than the creature of a county con-
federacy.[8] In such a political environment, aggressive expansion of
state agency responsibility is more likely to provoke debilitating
charges of empire building than to enhance agency power. Fear of adverse reaction thus increases the overall bureaucratic conservatism of
the state government and leads Parks and Forestry to cast a chary eye
toward any plans involving rapid expansion of responsibility, personnel, or maintenance expenses. Urban parks are labor- and mainte-
nance-intensive; their establishment means a sudden need to expand
personnel rolls and demand larger annual appropriations for operating expenses. Although it is frequently assumed that public bureaus
make maximizing appropriations their highest goal, there are some
situations when such a maximizing strategy is not appropriate.[9] This
appears to be such a case. Although the new expenses incurred as a
result of such acquisition would provide the rationale for increased
budget appropriations, they would be fixed, permanent expenses and
thus reduce the division's ability to weather New Jersey's all too frequent periods of fiscal retrenchment.

It is not surprising, then, to find that Parks and Forestry has espoused and acted in accordance with the hierarchical model of open
space responsibility and has avoided following a policy in keeping
with the interventionist model. In the mid-1960s, the division developed a long-range acquisition and development plan that is illustrative
of its thinking.[10] Although there was an effort to achieve a regional
balance, all the proposed new parks and expansions of existing ones
were in rural, low-density areas except for four facilities, one on
an urban site and three in suburban areas. The plan did not mention
access by public transportation nor discuss the client group to be

served, though both mode of transportation and client population were implicit in the discussion and evident in the architect's renderings of the facilities: The parking lots were large, and everyone was neatly dressed and en famille. Parks and Forestry still uses the 1967 plan as a planning blueprint and as a template against which to evaluate offerings. The plan, the model of state responsibility for open space it reflects, and the vision of the good life the plan is to promote still represent the bureaucratic ideology of Parks and Forestry and still provide the bases of its policy preferences.[11]

Acquiring Fish and Game Lands

The Division of Fish, Game, and Shellfisheries, commonly (and hereafter) referred to as Fish and Game, has been free of the policy choice that has confronted its sister division, Parks and Forestry. The operating environment of Fish and Game is very different from that of Parks and Forestry in several important ways, and the difference is reflected in its policies, problems, and prevailing attitudes. The division has the mixed blessing of a well-defined and articulate primary clientele, the state's hunting and fishing population. As in many states, Fish and Game's clients pay for most of its operating expenses through the purchase of hunting and fishing licenses;[12] and through the hunting clubs represented on the DEP's Advisory Fish and Game Council, the state's sportsmen give the division plenty of advice and criticism.[13] Wamsley and Zald point out that public organizations supported by user fees are frequently insensitive to any interests but those of their fee-paying clientele. Moreover, they frequently "enjoy a greater freedom from surveillance by superiors than those operating on general funds."[14] This has certainly been true for Fish and Game. Until recently, this fee arrangement freed it from assiduously courting legislative favor and allowed it to operate without much regard for those outside the hunting and fishing population. The operating environment of Fish and Game has really had two components: this small, articulate beneficiary group and the largely neutral public in which it is embedded. Such an environment has given Fish and Game a clear sense of mission and an associated acquisition policy free from the specter of plausible alternatives that has shadowed Parks and Forestry.

In evaluating tracts for possible addition to its holdings, Fish and Game takes several factors into consideration. First among them are intrinsic suitability for hunting and fishing, price, accessibility, local hunting laws, and contiguity to other holdings. Proximity to large population centers is of minor importance.[15] Indeed this proximity is usually negatively related to such positive factors as attractive price, freedom from hunting restrictions, and size of available parcel. The mobility of its clients is not a problem; most hunters and fishermen are nonurban and have access to automobiles.[16] As a result, Fish and Game has concentrated on acquiring rural property and has virtually no interest in urban or semiurban land.

The mission and consequent acquisition policy of Fish and Game confer several practical advantages on it. First, because its acquisitions are not scheduled for intensive recreational development, they do not arouse the intense local objections that those undertaken by Parks and Forestry occasionally encounter. A second advantage grows out of the fact that the land-holding units must depend on the annual appropriations of a fickle legislature for at least some of their expenses because maintenance costs are not covered by the Green Acres Program. Fortunately for Fish and Game, their land requires relatively little maintenance or development. This has meant that it can take advantage of Green Acres acquisition money to buy extensive tracts without worrying about a great increase in development and maintenance expenses. As a result of these advantages and because of aggressive leadership that, in the words of a former Parks and Forestry employee, allowed Fish and Game to "walk all over" his division,[17] Fish and Game got the lion's share of the money provided by the first Green Acres bond issue.

By the 1970s, however, Fish and Game's palmy days were over. Several trends worked to undermine its independence and security, and many of its previous advantages become liabilities. First, the division's clientele, the state's hunting and fishing population, remained static in size as the state's overall population increased. Legislative reapportionment in the late 1960s undermined the political power of this heavily rural client group.[18] The legislature, now more heavily representing urban and suburban constituents, came to ask whether such a small group should be the beneficiary of so much public largesse. Because it accepted for its acquisitions so much Green Acres money that ultimately came from the public-at-large, Fish and Game could no longer convincingly assert that its responsibilities did not extend beyond servicing hunters and fishermen. Then, with the rise of ecological consciousness, there evolved a second base of criticism of the division. State conservation groups like the Sierra Club and the New Jersey Conservation Foundation vocally took issue with many of its management policies aimed exclusively at the maintenance of game species. They argued that the division had a broader role in eco-system management than simply providing targets for hunters. As a result of these criticisms the division came to believe that it was con-tending with a general public increasingly unsympathetic to the divi-sion's definition of its mission.[19]

Casting about for a solution to these problems, Fish and Game con-sidered a program to extend interest in hunting and fishing among urbanites and suburban dwellers. Eventually, division administrators judged the program unrealistic, and it was never implemented. In response to criticism from environmentalists, the division added a nongame wildlife management section with responsibility for main-taining a state endangered-species list, issuing wildlife possession permits, and inspecting pet stores. The suspicion arises that the non-game section is little more than window dressing—an attempt to claim the state's entire population as beneficiaries while bowing to the ecological sensitivities of the times[20] and that it does not indicate a basic shift in goals.[21] The section has no say in land acquisition deci-sions, and its staff seems to be tolerated as a necessary evil by the rest of the division. The division has also claimed a land preservation role. As with Parks and Forestry, such a claim costs little and expands the range of rationales for the division's existence.

For Fish and Game there seems to be no choice of acquisition policy models. Although it has recently acquired the trappings of wider re-sponsibility for ecological management and hence for indirect service to the state's entire population, its basic commitment is to fish and game management. It is a commitment that leads to a logically co-herent policy of favoring large rural tracts and discounting considera-tions of mass accessibility. Open space for hunting and fishing is, by and large, immune to the dilemmas that bedevil general outdoor rec-reation planning, and freedom from such dilemmas has simplified decisions for Fish and Game.

This immunity is both a blessing and a threat. It has meant that the division has not been subjected to pressure to change its basic model of acquisition responsibility. Those who would push the state toward a more interventionist open space role have ignored the division. As a result, Fish and Game has not been charged with having an undue rural bias, as its sister division, Parks and Forestry, has been. On the other hand, it means that, when urban needs are deemed to be the first priority in the state, Fish and Game is an inappropriate instru-ment for dealing with these needs. A major shift toward state provision of urban open spaces, a move long advocated by state planners and occasionally favored by high state officials, would strongly reduce the division's importance.

The Office of Pineland Acquisitions

Recently, a new element has been added to the administrative machinery of the Green Acres Program, the Office of Pineland Acquisitions. For the last two decades, there has been rising interest in managing growth in the Pine Barrens, a region of more than 2,000 square miles of sparcely populated oak and pine woodland on New Jersey's infertile outer coastal plain, and a region into which the New York and Philadelphia metropolises have been steadily expanding. Recently this interest has lead to the passing of legislation and the establishment of government units with the potential for strong influence on the course of open space acquisition in the region. (The Pine Barrens is also called the Pinelands, an appelation of recent origin that seeks to avoid the negative connotations of "Barrens".)

From the 1930s onward, the state planners have been advocating an overall planning strategy for the region; and in the 1951 state development plan, they suggested that plans concentrate on preserving much of the area in a natural state.[22] In 1959, a weak intercounty planning board responsible for the Pine Barrens was established. Then in 1965, a scheme to put what would have been the world's largest airport in the middle of the region brought home the fact that it was the largest tract of undeveloped land in the New York–Washington corridor and that as such, its future was important to the entire mid-Atlantic conurbation, not just the local counties.[23] The following year the National Park Service began considering the Pine Barrens as the possible site of a national park or recreation area to serve the neighboring metropolitan areas and commissioned studies of the region's soil and drainage characteristics and of its biotic communities.[24] Although the Park Service saw many advantages to a national open space facility in the Pine Barrens, it failed to pursue the matter vigorously during the late sixties or early seventies. By then, however, the U.S. Department of Interior's Bureau of Outdoor Recreation had become interested in the future of the region. In 1975, it released a report, *The New Jersey Pine Barrens: Concepts for Preservation*, in which it recommended a preservation and growth management program involving the cooperation of local, state, and federal levels of government.

This report fueled the rising interest in the region and was soon followed by a series of government actions aimed at controlling the unregulated and accelerating growth of the Pine Barrens. New Jersey's congressional representatives introduced several bills in Congress that would give a measure of federal protection to much of the area. In 1977, New Jersey's Governor Brendan Byrne earmarked $10 million from the Green Acres fund for Pine Barren land acquisition by the state. In the same year the state's DEP allocated 25 percent of the money it was scheduled to receive from the federal government's LWCF to land purchases in the Pine Barrens. As an indication of local support for preservation of the region, the voters of Burlington County voted to acquire up to $1 million worth of conservation easements to protect threatened natural areas. Largely as a result of the efforts of New Jersey's citizens, congressional representatives, and the DEP, a bill establishing the Pinelands National Reserve was signed into law by President Carter in 1978.[25] It was the first area in the United States to be given national reserve status. The bill did not imply intention by the federal government to acquire in outright ownership of the entire area. Instead, the reserve designation was used to indicate that the future of the region was of national interest, so the federal government would have a hand in guiding its development. The bill allocated $23 million to the purchase of land in environmentally sensitive areas, allocated up to $3 million more to finance land-use planning, and called for the establishment of a planning body for the region.[26]

Shortly after the passage of the national legislation, the New Jersey legislature passed a complementary bill, the Pinelands Protection Act of 1979 (NJSA 13:18A–1 to 29). This bill authorized the establishment of the Pinelands Commission, an independent state commission made up of local, state, and federal representatives. The commission was to be the principal planning body for the region and as such was to assemble a large professional staff and draw up a comprehensive management plan. It also had general responsibility for regulating the activities of private development interests and coordinating the activities of the many units of local, county, and state government with an interest in the region.

Within the state DEP, the Office of Pineland Acquisitions was set up as the liaison unit between the DEP and the Pinelands Commission. The office was to draw up a list of properties the state should acquire, a list that would be compatible with the plans of the Pinelands Commission; and it was to establish as far as possible, a priority for acquiring the properties.[27]

Thus, the environment in which open space policy is made has recently become much richer with the creation of a large new planning unit, the Pinelands Commission; the formal expression of federal government interest in the future of a large region of the state; and the establishment within the DEP of a new unit exclusively assigned to open space acquisition. Yet these changes have not significantly altered the course of open space policy in the region, nor have they lessened the voice of the land-holding units in the Green Acres Program. If anything, the burgeoning interest in Pine Barrens planning has strengthened the position of the land-holding units in open space decision making. First, purchase initiative rests with the land-holding units. They have been the source of acquisition proposals for the Office of Pineland Acquisitions because it is a small unit without the staff capacity to work up detailed proposals. It has to depend on units of the state government that do have the capacity—the land-holding units. The office's capacity for an independent policy stance is thus reduced. To date, all of the acquisitions made through the Office of Pineland Acquisitions have come from proposals by the land-holding units.[28] A second source of power for the land-holding units is that they manage any tract eventually acquired by the state. This gives them the authority to review proposals from any source for management considerations. Does the tract present special maintenance problems? Does the land-holding unit have the resources to administer it properly?[29] The importance of such considerations in the thinking of the land-holding units can be seen in the fact that all twenty proposals they submitted to the Governor's Pinelands Review Committee (an advisory committee charged with devising strategies to preserve the region) were adjacent to lands already held by the state. In most cases the proposals eliminated private holdings surrounded by state land, consolidated separate state holdings, or smoothed out border irregularities.[30]

Although the Pinelands Commission has considerable power over the disposition of federal open space money allocated to the region inasmuch as it must approve purchases involving federal funds, it has no formal voice in state acquisitions made exclusively with Green Acres money. Furthermore, its plans do not differ much from those of the land-holding units.[31] Most of the acquisition proposals put forth in its *Draft Comprehensive Management Plan* were drawn up with the close cooperation of the land-holding units of the DEP.[32] The Pinelands Commission is willing to make management considerations primary in shaping its list of acquisition recommendations, and there seem to be few basic points of difference between the commission staff and the land-holding units.[33]

In sum, although the increasing interest in the future of the Pine Barrens has resulted in new units with an interest in open space policy and more public funds, it has neither altered the land-holding units' predispositions nor lessened their ability to propose purchases or influence acquisitions. If anything, the interest in preserving the Pine Barrens has given the rural acquisitions that land-holding units prefer a patina of ecological responsibility, while the additional money has enabled them to acquire land in this area faster than otherwise possible. In fact, one person familiar with the Pine Barrens suggested that the land-holding units benefited so much from the new interest in the region that their directors ought to have their titles changed to "the Pine Barren Barons."

Open Space and the Goals of the State Planners

That planners in the state government have long been involved in open space planning is clear from the numerous plans and reports in which a succession of state planning units proposed a policy of more active state open space acquisition over the years from 1930 to 1960.[34] Personnel from the State Planning Board's successor, the Division of State and Regional Planning (DSRP), conducted the study, then wrote the report, *The Need for a State Recreational Land Acquisition and Development Program*, that outlined the Green Acres Program and triggered legislative action on the original bond referendum bill. The land-holding units, especially Parks and Forestry, resented, nonetheless, the planners' involvement in open space in general and in the Green Acres Program in particular. Parks and Forestry believed planners understood neither its problems nor the practical side of open space management. According to one planner, "Parks and Forestry just didn't trust us."[35]

The matter of trust aside, there were intrinsic points of friction between the DSRP and Parks and Forestry that grew out of their differing views of the state's open space responsibility. The DSRP was charged with the following tasks:

To assemble and analyze facts pertaining to the development of New Jersey;
To prepare and maintain a comprehensive state development plan and capital improvements program;

To strive for fuller coordination of the development activities of the several
state departments;

To stimulate, assist, and coordinate municipal, county and regional planning
activities;

To administer planning assistance programs under which state or federal
funds are made available for urban planning.[36]

DSRP emphasis was on intergovernment coordination, comprehensive planning, and an integrated approach to problem solving. As a result, whereas Parks and Forestry tended to see the Green Acres Program in straightforward terms as a financing system for the state's parks and forests, the DSRP tended to see it as a tool with which to attack what it had identified as the state's major planning problems: the lack of comprehensive development planning and the deterioration of the cities. Given their point of view and sense of mission, it was not surprising, then, that planners came to see the interventionist model of state open space responsibility as the proper one, for it fit into their broader notions of the state's responsibility for its cities. As DSRP was not involved in the administration of open space, it was, as the land-holding units claimed, less sensitive to the practical drawbacks of the interventionist model.[37] The planners believed that, as the one unit of state government charged with thinking comprehensively about major problems, they had a right to a strong voice in shaping the policies of programs that could be used in solving those problems.[38]

The DSRP tried to push Parks and Forestry into more urban acquisitions. Parks and Forestry resented what it considered to be planning's unjustified meddling in its own area of responsibility and expertise.[39] As a result, tensions and conflict developed between the two divisions. As a sister division to the land-holding units rather than an agency with a formal position of authority over them, DSRP's efforts at influencing policy could only increase Parks and Forestry's resentment and exacerbate tension between the two divisions.[40]

From the very beginning of the Green Acres Program, the DSRP tried to use the meetings of the Land Use Committee to espouse its views and guide policy, but several factors operated strongly to undercut its position. First, it appeared that the planners misunderstood how deeply rooted both in self-interest and in notions of its proper role were the policy preferences of Parks and Forestry. Planning thought that persuasion would be the mode of interaction on the committee; and this being the case, their broad perspective would have to prevail.[41] It did not. Land offerings were usually made directly to Parks and Forestry, so inertia and initiative were on its side. Deliberations usually involved specific acquisition requests submitted by the land-holding units to the committee for its consideration, and Parks and Forestry managed to keep discussion centered on the technical merits of the tracts in question. It seldom allowed discussion to wander into more general policy areas. Within this narrow context, its requests were usually well justified. The prices were right; the tracts were attractive; the user demand was there; the development plan was well thought out. Planning continually found itself saying, "Yes, but. . . ." Second, although Fish and Game and Parks and Forestry had somewhat overlapping roles and sometimes subjected each other's proposals to close technical scrutiny, their behavior on the committee usually tended to be accommodating and cooperative toward each other.[42] "You support my project, and I will support yours" was the norm. The DSRP, on the other hand, lacked allies.

Yet another factor came to work against planning. When the Green Acres Program was established, the state was determined to keep administration costs as low as possible, lest it be charged with spending on salaries and office supplies what should have gone into land purchases. As a result, the acquisition unit's staff was kept to a minimum. Yet demands for quick acquisition of "fast disappearing" open space came from both the press and the program's legislative backers. Caught in the squeeze, the unit became very sensitive to the amount of work involved in making an acquisition and strove to keep its workload to a minimum. On occasion the state has even withdrawn from an acquisition, not because of lack of money, but because the state Green Acres office thought it lacked sufficient staff to handle all the work involved.[43] Urban parks frequently involve multiple acquisitions, protracted negotiations, and a wealth of time-consuming details. Rural tracts, on the other hand, usually take relatively few manhours to process and can be quickly dispatched by a small staff. It was not surprising, then, that the acquisition unit developed a strong bias for rural acquisition and came to look with disfavor on urban acquisition proposals, opposing them almost reflexively.

In meetings of the Land Use Committee and its successor within the DEP, the head of the state Green Acres office could be counted on to be sympathetic with Parks and Forestry's rural bias and to resist efforts to force the state into an interventionist role. Such a role would have put his unit in the center of a double bind. The increased workload would bring acquisition progress to a crawl, but an expanded staff would put an unfavorable tilt on the ratio of overhead expenses to acquisition costs and perhaps, as a consequence, endanger the program.

The DSRP suffered another strong disadvantage on which the land-holding units could capitalize in rejecting its suggestions. The tendency of those who oppose planners' suggestions to label planners pejoratively as dreamers, idealists, and "superman planners" is no doubt common; and unfortunately, the division had acquired within the state government a reputation for impracticality.[44] Kolesar, discussing the division's problems, writes that "the Division of State and Regional Planning had a solid rating within its profession but wore the standard 'dreamer' label pinned on planners by outsiders."[45] Its advocacy of an expanded role for the state in the provision of urban open space supported this image. Because such a course would be expensive and would involve many administrative and maintenance problems, the land-holding units said the planners did not understand the practical considerations involved in open space policy making.[46] The planners further exacerbated their image problems by producing proposals for urban open space in which there was little thought given to the costs or the necessary sequence of steps involved in proposal implementation. The planners argued, justifiably perhaps, that such matters were the concern of the land-holding units because they had the expertise to deal with them. Nevertheless, the damage to the planners' reputation was done.[47]

Having found it could not use the Land Use Committee to effect its ends, planning failed either to change the rules by which the committee made its recommendations or to find a way to circumvent the committee. Although like most planning units the DSRP had no line authority, no money or favors to dispense, and no base of independent power, it did have a powerful piece of what Freeman calls "supporting artillery"—the support and trust of succeeding governors who viewed many of planning's goals as in keeping with the overall goals of their administrations.[48] Unfortunately for the DSRP, it did not use this support effectively. When it realized its weak position on the Land Use Committee, it appealed to the governor to ask the land-holding units to listen to what they, the planners, had to say. The governor did this but to no avail. Perhaps if the DSRP had realized the magnitude of the differences between its aims for open space policy and those of the land-holding units, it would have used its access to the governor to obtain a bargaining chip for use on the Land Use Committee—veto power, for example. It did not. Apparently the planners, who had little previous experience in policy formation, never lost their misplaced faith in reasoning and persuasion.

In 1967, in the middle of planning's conflicts with Parks and Forestry the state created the Department of Community Affairs (DCA).

Although avowedly the department dealt with "total community de-velopment" whether urban, suburban, or rural,[49] it was created in the aftermath of the urban rioting of the mid-1960s and, according to one of the department's high officials, "it saw its constituency as the cit-ies."[50] The planning division was taken out of the DCED and became part of the newly formed DCA. This move further weakened the planning division's ability to influence open space policy. Putting the planning unit in a department with avowedly urban interests did not change the unit's ideas about open space; they were pro-urban to be-gin with. Now, however, the DSRP reported to a different commis-sioner, one for whom urban problems were a major concern but who had little interest in using state open space policy as an instrument for dealing with them. As a consequence, public open space was a minor concern for the new department within which the DSRP found itself. Although the DSRP continued to be represented on the Land Use Committee, when it spoke, it spoke as an outsider and what it said was taken to represent the views of the new department in which it found itself.[51] It was a department that, by its imposing and aggressive tactics, soon made many enemies.[52] Whereas previously the planners' opposition to the state's open space policies had been at least some-what tolerated as all-in-the-family criticism, it was now deeply re-sented as the unwarranted intrusion of an abrasive department.

In 1970 the DCED itself was broken up, with the land-holding units and the Green Acres administrative offices becoming part of the newly formed DEP. Now the Green Acres Program found itself within the broad context of the "environmental problem," the unifying con-cern of the new department. Because planning had the "urban prob-lem" as its organizational context, the DEP considered planning's legitimate interest in the Green Acres Program to be reduced to what it saw as the very small intersection of the two problems.[53] Fur-thermore, as Allison observes with reference to interagency power struggles, unsuccessful investment of energy in losing causes de-pletes both the morale and the reputation.[54] By the mid-1970s, the DSRP's involvement with the Green Acres Program had depleted both and disinclined it from further jousting with the land-holding units. As a result of both situations, contact between the DEP and the DSRP on open space matters became less and less frequent.

Partly in response to the loss of contact with the DSRP and partly to co-opt its role, the DEP set up its own unit with responsibility for open space planning, especially recreational open space planning. The unit was attached to the Green Acres administrative unit and was charged with the tasks of coordinating open space planning for the various land-holding units. Ironically, this new planning unit soon developed an antagonistic relationship with the land-holding units like that of the DSRP. The recreational planning unit, like the DSRP before it, takes a strongly urban, interventionist position. It believes the state's open space responsibility to all its citizens requires special considerations of some of them, namely those urban dwellers who are disadvantaged by traditional policy. Its arguments are similar to some of those put forth by DSRP and are similarly dismissed by the land-holding units.

That such an antagonism could develop all over again, and in rough-ly the same form, supports a conclusion that the conflict between open space planners and open space administrators goes beyond per-sonalities and specific situations. For the planners, freedom from practical considerations growing out of management responsibilities allows attitudes to be shaped by unrestricted considerations of the state's major problems and by prevailing norms of urban respon-sibility. This in turn encourages what Poland calls strategic planning, planning that first identifies fundamental goals and needs and then goes about marshaling the necessary resources to meet them.[55] For the open space administrators, practical considerations are foremost; administrative goals and perhaps even moral norms are shaped to fit logistic considerations and available resources. This difference in atti-tudes is reflected in a perceptive comment by the head of the DEP's recreation planning unit: "I look at the problem as one of getting rec-reation opportunities to people who need them. I think that the ur-ban park proposals were basically good ideas although they were not well thought out."[56] Referring to Parks and Forestry's opposition to the proposed parks, he said, "Parks and Forestry didn't like them; they would have been difficult to manage, and in a way I understand their point of view. After all, they think of themselves as land man-agers." This perceived difference in planners' and managers' criteria for success is strikingly similar to that found by Needleman and Nee-dleman. "Community planners perceive a fundamental contradiction between their goals and those of operating agencies. Operating agen-cies, they feel, tend to measure success quantitatively in terms of how much they can produce at the least cost in the least amount of time. Community planners, on the other hand, measure success qualita-tively in terms of how well community needs and desires have been satisfied."[57]

Thus, for reasons rooted in expedience, routine, and a sense of professional mission, the hierarchical model came to be favored by the state's open space managers; and the managers, rather than the planners, got their way. Above both of them, however, was the DEP commissioner, and ultimate administrative responsibility for open space policy rested with him.

The Role of the Commissioner

The commissioner, a member of the state cabinet, is the bridge between professional open space administrators and elected political authority. He is an appointee chosen by the governor and serving at the governor's pleasure. He has a great deal of formal authority over the Green Acres Program, and with that authority he has the power to shape state open space policy. He can appoint and replace the Green Acres Program administrator and the heads of the land-holding units. The Green Acres office personnel are his subordinates. All grant requests coming from the land-holding units and approved by the Land Use Committee must, in turn, have his approval.

There are two opposite ways the commissioner can view his role in the Green Acres Program. In the first view, he sees himself as a passive overseer of a bureaucratic process that works properly only when left largely alone. His role within this view is that of a protector of his department's decision-making autonomy and a buffer against political interference from outside. The second view is a more active one that concedes less legitimacy (and less integrity) to the bureaucratic process. Here, the bureaucracy must be strongly guided, controlled, and made responsive to higher authority if it is to perform satisfactorily and not simply seek its own self-serving ends. Within this view, the commissioner sees himself as a conduit into the program for demands from higher, elected authorities; or he sees himself as the proper source of all policy decisions, which he may then have to force on his subordinates.

Usually the commissioner is disinclined to immerse himself deeply in open space policy. He has many other responsibilities, some far removed from open space policy and usually some that are more pressing. The commissioner of the DCED had promoting industrial growth and overseeing state planning among his responsibilities. The commissioner of the DEP is responsible for pollution regulation and the maintenance of air and water quality. These matters usually occupy the greater part of the commissioner's attention, leaving what is left over for less important, or at least less pressing, open space concerns.

The fact that the commissioner is stretched so thin by his other responsibilities makes it advantageous for him to adopt the first, more passive role as the protector or buffer for subordinates who make as many decisions as possible. It means he can allow the program to run itself with little personal attention except on those special occasions when his intervention is necessary to preserve his department's integrity or autonomy. March and Simon suggest that a high administrator's lack of concern for all but the most generalized problems his organization faces is administratively rational behavior because, "as we move upwards in the supervisory and executive hierarchy, the range of interrelated matters over which an individual has purview becomes larger and larger, more and more complex. The growing complexity of the problems can only be matched against the finite powers of the individual if the problem is dealt with in grosser and more aggregate forms."[58] According to this argument, detached behavior was rational for a commissioner, given the range and complexity of his responsibilities. Commissioners Robert Roe and Richard Sullivan, who between them have overseen the Green Acres Program for much of its life, tended to act as buffers; and for Sullivan, at least, the choice of this role was a conscious one. These commissioners protected the land-holding units and the program's steering committee, defending them when necessary from external criticism and deflecting special demands made on them from outside.

The changes these commissioners forced on their subordinates were largely tactical or co-optive ones designed to blunt or defuse opposition to the Green Acres Program rather than to redirect the program toward new goals. In the early 1960s, Commissioner Roe, to head off criticism from the state cranberry growers, prohibited the land-holding units from acquiring any cranberry land except that which had come on the market without prompting. The state would not seek out owners and try to persuade them to sell, nor would it resort to condemnation. In the late 1960s, the Department of Agriculture, fearing that Green Acres purchases of working farmland would accelerate the decline of agriculture in the state, asked the DEP commissioner to refrain from acquiring any land in agriculture by condemnation. The commissioner complied by issuing an administrative directive prohibiting such agricultural takings; and at his prompting, the prohibition was written into the 1971 bond authorization bill.

When local opposition to an acquisition was intense and came to bear on the governor or the local legislators, the commissioner would instruct the land acquisition unit to proceed slowly or to put the project into inactive status until the controversy died down. Conversely, if there were strong local demand for a particular tract, he would encourage the unit to move quickly and give the acquisition a high priority. According to Sullivan, during his term of office, outside pressure never either killed an acquisition or forced a land-holding unit to make one its staff considered unjustifiable by its professional criteria.[59]

Very little of the activity of these commissioners touched on questions of the basic role of the state in providing open space. Sullivan actively disavowed such an involvement; he considered it a matter for the professionals on his staff. He saw his job as taking acquisition projects on a "wish list" compiled by the land-holding units and guiding them through the rocks and whirlpools of political life. His major concern was to avoid alienating the public or the politicians and to prevent any major scandals over shady land dealings.[60] Even though Sullivan's predecessor, Roe, had a reputation as a "strong" commissioner who made many policy decisions himself,[61] he, like Sullivan, usually depended on his staff to generate the acquisition proposals, and he interfered little in the process. A sense of being defenders of the Green Acres Program and of what Freeman called "strategic sensitivity" to generalized demands for efficiency in public programs led both of these commissioners to the same conclusion as Parks and Forestry about urban acquisitions, i.e., such acquisitions were unwise.[62] They meant many nonurban acquisitions forgone, and their per-acre costs made them look bad in the light of public scrutiny.

Sullivan's successor, David Bardin, took a very different view of the land-holding units and his role in the Green Acres Program. Personally flamboyant and energetic, he disliked career bureaucrats, and he tended to view the Green Acres administrators as bureaucrats who had grown into the habit of making open space policy for their own convenience under his predecessors. Bardin took a personal interest in policy making and immersed himself in the details of the Green Acres Program's operation. Soon after becoming commissioner he took several steps to increase his direct control over open space policy and fund allocation. To correct what he saw as a serious downward leakage of authority under the previous commissioners,[63] he deactivated the advisory committee and personally assumed its role in evaluating requests from the land-holding units. He centralized the receipt and evaluation of unsolicited offerings within the DEP's land acquisition unit, so that the land-holding units could no longer receive offerings; they had to refer them directly to the land acquisition unit. He demanded information rather than decisions from his subordinates. He seldom asked for proposals or opinions from the land-holding units.

Clearly, he opted for the second role open to a commissioner, that of active policy maker.[64] When the state had the opportunity to acquire Ramapo Mountain, a large tract in Bergen County accessible to the urbanized northeastern corner of the state, Parks and Forestry was not enthusiastic about the opportunity. It judged the tract to be too expensive and of purely local interest. Bardin overruled the division. Indeed, he scarcely listened to it before committing the DEP to the purchase. Shortly afterward Bardin approved the purchase of a small tract of wetlands in the Hackensack Meadows over the objection of Parks and Forestry. He announced that it would be developed as a state park to serve the urban areas surrounding the meadow, although Parks and Forestry maintained that the tract was too small for the state to manage effectively.[65]

Even when a commissioner wants change, however, there are practical limits to his ability to force it on a reluctant bureaucracy. As Fox points out, bureaucrats have a wide range of resources with which to resist the orders of superiors who wish to reorient bureau policy.[66] Perhaps most important, they control information. The hierarchical organization of state bureaucracy operates to limit the effective power of the commissioner because the information he needs to make decisions frequently comes from underlings with a vested interest in the decision outcomes. Commissioner Bardin found himself in the position of trying to undercut the autonomy of the land-holding units while relying on them for the information with which to do it. Although Bardin strove mightily to familiarize himself with the routines and processes of his department,[67] he could only infrequently take the initiative from its divisions. Although he had a reputation as a man who liked to take the initiative himself, his decisions on open space acquisitions were, with few exceptions (like those already mentioned), limited to choices presented to him by his subordinates. An official of Fish and Game said of Bardin, "When you come right down to it, he was just like Sullivan [the former commissioner] in the way he depended on us for acquisition proposals. Only he [Bardin] was more suspicious of us and rejected more of our proposals."[68] Sharkansky thinks the situation in which Commissioner Bardin found himself is a common one; because administrators have a virtual monopoly of detailed and technical information, superiors may be in a position to accept or reject their suggestions, but they are seldom in a position to initiate counter proposals.[69] Crozier goes so far as to say that, in the face of opposition from within, the superior is, in most cases, as helpless as his authority is absolute.[70] Although certainly not helpless, a commissioner who seeks to force changes in the face of the strong contrary preferences of the land-holding units must show extreme persistence. The case of Liberty Park, briefly recounted here, shows both what it takes to force change and why such efforts are so rare.

Liberty Park, a park created on approximately 600 acres of derelict Jersey City waterfront facing the Statue of Liberty, was first proposed in the early sixties as a catalyst for the renovation of downtown Jersey City. From the beginning Parks and Forestry opposed the idea, claiming the park would be too expensive to acquire, develop, and maintain and, because it would be an urban park, would be an inappropriate addition to the state park system. The commissioners, backed by three succeeding governors, supported the park project nonetheless and took strong personal interest in it, making sure acquisitions and development plans proceeded on schedule. The park became a symbol of the state's commitment to its cities; and each succeeding administration adopted a high-level, ongoing interest in it. Even Commissioner Sullivan, who normally let his land-holding units assign their own priorities, kept Parks and Forestry from dragging their feet on Liberty Park's development.[71] Finally, in the face of continual pressure, Parks and Forestry accepted the park. It rationalized that Liberty Park was not just an urban park in Jersey City but, because of its strategic location across from the Statue of Liberty, a park of national importance.[72] On such terms it accepted the inevitable.

The Geography of State Open Space Acquisitions

Because the administrators in the land-holding units have dominated the acquisition process, excluding the planners from an effective voice and neutralizing most of the occasional attempts by commissioners to force change, it stands to reason that the pattern of direct state acquisitions made through the Green Acres Program should reflect the hierarchical model that the land-holding units so strongly favored.

As Table 3 shows, in the early sixties, before the Green Acres Program, state-owned open spaces were strongly concentrated in the state's low-density, exurban areas. They were primarily in the pine woodlands and salt marshes of southern New Jersey and in the wooded, hilly uplands to the northwest. The advent of the Green Acres Program did nothing to make inexpensive, infertile rural land less economically or politically attractive to a state land-holding unit; nor did it change the state's open space decision makers' views of state responsibilities. Not surprisingly, then, state acquisitions made through the Green Acres Program (also shown in Table 3) tended to

Table 3. State-owned Open Space by County

County	1961		Acquired 1962–1974	
	Acreage	Percentage of total	Acreage	Percentage of total
Atlantic	19,800	7.0	3,272	3.1
Bergen	1,900	.7	358	.4
Burlington	98,521	34.8	8,698	8.0
Camden	15,521	5.4	244	.2
Cape May	11,209	4.0	25,736	25.2
Cumberland	33,265	11.7	5,537	5.4
Essex	0	.0	205	.2
Gloucester	2,349	.8	2,068	2.1
Hudson	12	.0	310	.3
Hunterdon	7,864	2.8	526	.5
Mercer	1,215	.4	1,161	1.2
Middlesex	1,031	.4	241	.2
Monmouth	2,367	.8	8,227	8.8
Morris	2,459	.9	3,707	3.6
Ocean	36,310	12.8	10,429	10.2
Passaic	5,253	1.9	8,602	8.2
Salem	4,601	1.6	2,782	2.8
Somerset	522	.2	808	.7
Sussex	31,223	11.0	15,346	15.0
Union	0	.0	0	.0
Warren	7,500	2.6	3,735	3.6
Total	282,924	99.8	101,992	99.7

SOURCE: "New Jersey Green Acres History Goes Back Twelve Years," *New Jersey Environmental Times*, October 1971, p. 6, and the New Jersey Department of Environmental Protection, various internal documents.

NOTE: Because of rounding off, percentages do not equal 100.

repeat and reinforce the preexisting pattern. The densely populated counties of Union, Hudson, Camden, and Bergen have had less than 300 acres of state Green Acres acquisition while thinly populated Cape May, Ocean, and Sussex counties each have had more than 10,000 acres of state acquisition.

The program was used to add considerable acreage to the state's three largest open space units, the Wharton and Lebanon Forests in the Pine Barrens of southern New Jersey and Stokes Forest in the northwest. Large, new wetland holdings were added along the Atlantic coast and the coast of the Delaware Bay. Large tracts were added in the forested highlands of Passaic, Morris, and Sussex counties as additions to preexisting holdings or as new open space units. Map 1 shows the state's major Green Acres acquisition projects, those whose authorized expenditure was over $.5 million. (It does not show local purchases made with Green Acres grants-in-aid.) Except for six, these major purchases are in areas remote from the state's centers of population. Three of the six—Great Peace Meadow, Ramapo Mountain, and Ronconcas Creek—are on the outer periphery of a metropolitan area; and two of the six—Ramapo Mountain and Liberty Park—were acquired over the strenuous objections of Parks and Forestry.

Correlating population density of a county with amount of Green Acres state-acquired open space within it produces a correlation coefficient (r) of $-.69$.[73] It is a strong negative correlation, and it shows the degree to which the state has avoided purchases in areas of population concentration. If anything, the correlation using the county as the unit of analysis understates the strength of the bias, for within counties the acquisitions are usually in low-density areas. For example, the southeastern section of Passaic County contains the large cities of Passaic, Clifton, and Paterson, which give the county a high mean density. The northwestern sector of the county, the site of all the state's Green Acres acquisitions, is lightly populated, however.

As the result of this acquisition bias, the state's open space holdings have remained overwhelmingly rural and strongly reflect the hierarchical model of state open space responsibility. Maps 2 and 3 pinpoint the holdings of the state's land-holding units. Map 2 shows state forests, parks, and recreation areas. More than half of them are in the rural northwestern section of the state, and most of the others are in thinly populated areas to the south. Map 3 shows Fish and Game holdings. Although a rural pattern prevails here too, the holdings are more concentrated in the southern part of the state, especially on the Outer Coastal Plain and in the wetlands along the Atlantic Ocean and Delaware Bay.

Looking at state acquisitions by minor civil divisions in which they occur provides another gauge of the extent of rural acquisitions. Using a classification scheme developed by the state's DCA, New Jersey's municipalities are divided into urban, suburban, and rural groups.[74] Map 4 shows the locations of the three types of municipalities, and Table 4 shows the number and percentage of towns within each group that have state open spaces within their borders. The one state open space unit in an urban municipality is Liberty Park. Within the suburban group, most of the state land holdings are in the newer, lower-density suburbs; and frequently acquisition preceded suburbanization. In sum, there can be no doubt that under the dominance of the

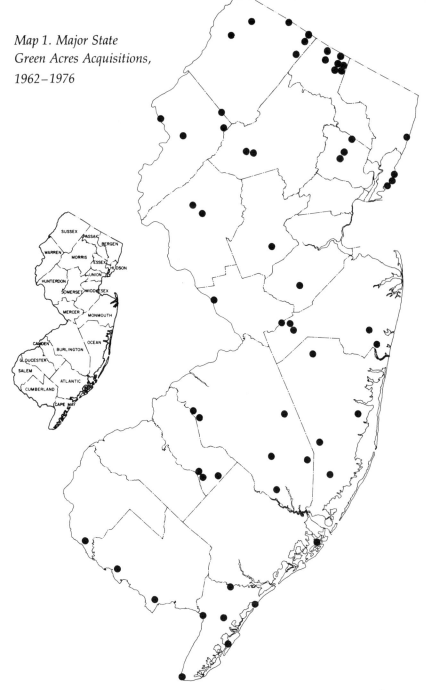

*Map 1. Major State
Green Acres Acquisitions,
1962–1976*

SOURCE: New Jersey Department of Environmental Protection, "Green Acres Quarterly Summary of Completed and Active Projects," April 1977.

NOTES: The symbols in Map 1 show the locations of the tracts of land acquired through the Green Acres Program. Because those in Maps 2 and 3 represent the administrative units into which the acquisitions have been incorporated, there is an imperfect match between Map 1 on one hand and Maps 2 and 3 on the other. For example, several acquisitions in lower Burlington County, each individually represented on Map 1, are subsumed on Map 2 into the symbol for Wharton State Forest, the administrative unit into which they were incorporated.

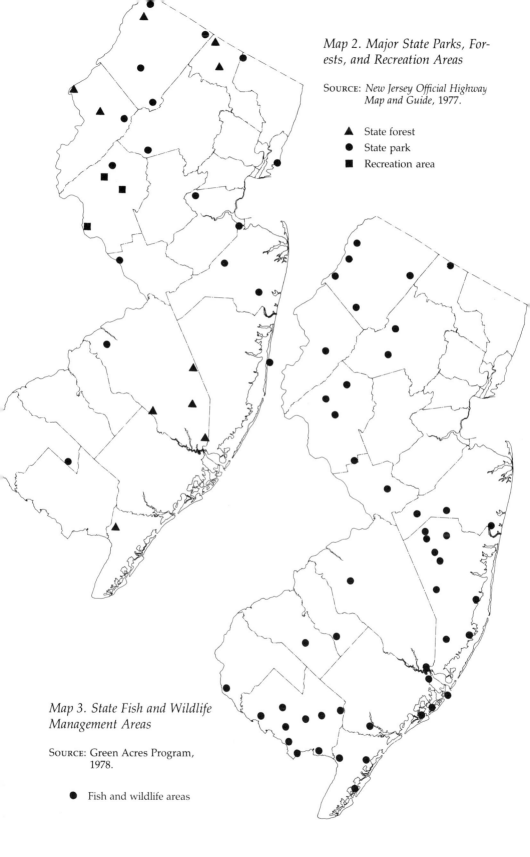

*Map 2. Major State Parks, For-
ests, and Recreation Areas*

Source: *New Jersey Official Highway
Map and Guide, 1977.*

▲ State forest
● State park
■ Recreation area

*Map 3. State Fish and Wildlife
Management Areas*

Source: Green Acres Program,
1978.

● Fish and wildlife areas

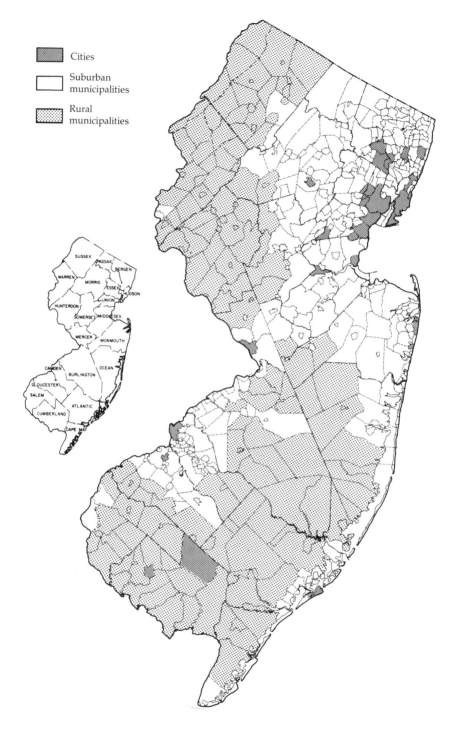

Map 4. Municipalities According to Degree of Urbanization in 1972

SOURCE: New Jersey Department of Community Affairs, Division of State and Regional Planning, *New Jersey Municipal Profiles: Intensity of Urbanization*, Trenton, 1972.

Table 4. State Acquisitions by Type of Municipality in Which They Occur

	Number of municipalities		
	In group	With state-owned open space	Percentage of municipalities within group with state-owned open space
Urban	31	1	3
Suburban	315	19	6
Rural	221	54	24
Total	567	74	

SOURCE: New Jersey Department of Community Affairs, *Municipal Workbook Number 8*, 1972.

land-holding units the state section of the Green Acres Program has had a rural bias. These data attest not only to its existence but to its considerable strength.

Far from denying that there is such a bias, the land-holding units agree that it exists. They hold that such a bias is proper and in keeping with their missions. Fish and Game holds that given its conservation responsibilities, its clientele, and the activities for which it provides facilities, anything but a rural acquisitions bias would be foolishness. Parks and Forestry argues that at the center of their responsibility lies, first, the provision of statewide recreational facilities that are predominantly resource-based and, second, the preservation of natural systems of statewide interest. Such responsibilities, they argue, lead them along a chain of irrefutable logic to an acquisition policy that favors rural, low-density acquisitions.

When, in 1975, the state legislature's Division of Program Analysis criticized the Green Acres Program for promoting excessive rural acquisitions,[75] the program's administrators replied that such criticism was unfair because the program analysts looked only at direct state acquisitions. The administrators contended that, had the analysts looked at the local grants program as well, they would have found a complementary bias toward cities and suburbs that counterbalanced the biases of the direct state acquisitions. The program's administrators were correct. An examination of the dynamics of the local grants section of the Green Acres Program explains why this counterbalancing took place.

5

The Local Matching Fund

Administering the Fund

Soon after the passage of the first Green Acres bond referendum, the local grant section of the Office of Real Estate and Legal Services was established to handle the details of administering the local matching grant program.[1] It was to be the state's contact unit with New Jersey's lower levels of government. In theory, the state, through the Office of Legal Services and Real Estate and the Land Use Committee, was to exercise considerable control over the direction of the local matching grant program. The local grant section was to advise local governments informally, while their requests were still in the formulative stages, about the suitability of proposed acquisitions. Once a formal request was made, the Land Use Committee and its successor, the DEP Advisory Committee on Open Land Conservation, were empowered to evaluate the request against the goals of the program and either approve or disapprove it. Finally, an application had to have the approval of the commissioner himself.

In practice, the state has exercised little effective control over the direction of the local matching grant program. As with the state direct acquisition program, the important decision making has become decentralized and has diffused away from where it formally belongs. In this program it is diffused among the local government units, making the program almost completely user controlled in fact, although not by design. Let me explain why this took place and what the consequences have been.

While the Green Acres local program was being formulated, there was an assumption of great latent demand for open space funds among the state's counties and municipalities because of the Regional Plan Association's (RPA) study showing a great lack of open space provided by local and county governments. Such a latent demand would mean that a state grants-in-aid program would be distributing a scarce resource, making necessary a restrictive allocation procedure to insure a just distribution of funds.[2] Inasmuch as it was unlikely that there would be enough money to accommodate all requests, a formula was chosen whereby a municipality or a county could apply for an amount limited by its population—the larger the population, the higher the grant ceiling. For reasons discussed later, the expected rush for the money never materialized; grant applications came in dribs and drabs. (The program began with the expectation that the local matching fund would be depleted in less than three years; because of the slow rate at which applications were received, it took six.) As a result the Green Acres program discarded the formula and lifted its grant ceiling. The official rationale for the action was that the ceiling might prohibit the acquisition of large, attractive tracts of regional interest if they happened to be located in towns with small populations.[3] Clearly this was undeniable, but the lifting of the ceiling largely resulted from a realization that the local Green Acres fund was not a limited resource in an immediate sense; there was plenty of money to go around in the face of less-than-anticipated demand.

This lack of immediate demand produced an awkward situation for the program's backers and administrators. The referendum campaign had convinced the legislature and the public at large that there was an open space "crisis" and that the state had to move quickly to help local governments acquire land before it was developed or before prices become prohibitive. Now, sluggish demand brought pressure on the local program administrators to spend money quickly, first to show that there really was an open space crisis and, second, to show that they were doing something about it. Their main problem, it turned out, was one of promoting increased demand, not restricting it or selectively meeting it. Lifting of restrictions meant that the important decisions came to be made below the state level, in the county and municipal governments that were considering applying for Green Acres money. To this day, the state's local matching program administrators largely confine their decisions to procedural matters such as whether an application is complete or all supporting documents are in order. Because of the interests of its constituent members, the Land Use Committee has concentrated its attention on state acquisitions and been considerably less concerned with the local program, thus removing another possible source of active state policy making on local grants-in-aid.

There is, however, an informal evaluation procedure that centers largely on technical matters. When an application is received from a local government, Green Acres local grant personnel look at the site and the development plans, then advise the local government on such matters as the suitability of the terrain for its intended use, the adequacy of access routes, the appropriateness of proposed facilities. If the site and development plans are satisfactory, approval of the grant is virtually automatic. Of the more than one thousand grant requests handled by the local section, only one has been turned down formally, and fewer than a dozen have been informally rejected before they reached the final application stage.[4] Consequently, the configuration of the program's results is not due in any measure to a specific state distribution policy; rather, it is the result of hundreds of local decisions that, having been made, trigger state spending and thus shape the program.

Because the Green Acres local program administrators are dealing with what is virtually an unlimited resource and because pressures incline them to encourage distribution rather than restrict it, they are in a fortunate public relations position. They can keep application procedures extremely simple, and they can make great efforts to be helpful to all local applicants. These efforts are not lost on local government personnel. The local office is highly regarded among them; and without exception, the municipal and county officials I interviewed said that the Green Acres local grants office was the most efficient and helpful unit of state government they had encountered. Within the local office the atmosphere is relaxed and friendly; the administrators seem to enjoy their work and derive satisfaction from helping their clients. They are hardly the neutral, dispassionate bureaucrats of the Weberian stereotype.[5] As one local program administrator told me, "Sure we're nice guys, but then it's easy when your job is to give away money."[6]

When the development proviso was added to the Green Acres Program in 1974, a separate unit of the local grants office was established to process requests for development aid. Most of the requests came from cities, many of which needed a great deal of advice and help in preparing the necessary forms, as simple as they were; and the unit's personnel gladly gave much time and effort to assisting them. They believed it to be part of their job to be more than neutral evaluators of these applications, that they owed cities that extra bit of attention and concern. By 1974, special concern for the cities had become part of the prevailing ideology of state service, and the attitude of the Green Acres personnel handling development grants fit neatly into it. Blau's point that ideological identification with progressive goals can go hand in hand with bureaucratic self-interest is very much the case with the Green Acres local grants unit.[7] By offering extra help to the cities, the unit is expanding its service role in a noncontroversial manner and in just the direction dictated by a progressive ideology of government responsibility. Simon, Smithburg, and Thompson write that "a source of tremendous value to some groups are the social values they believe they are promoting through their work."[8] For Green Acres local grant personnel, the value promoted is service to a previously underserved segment of the state's population, which appears to be a genuine source of job satisfaction for them.

The Green Acres local grant office maintains its accommodating attitude toward all applicants; yet it offers extra interest and effort to the cities. Thus it pleases everyone. A public official in Newark said, "The Green Acres people in Trenton are great. They have a sincere interest in Newark; they're not like HUD."[9] Yet the chairman of the park commission of an affluent exurban county said that Green Acres personnel understood that open space meant nature, not asphalt. Because there is so little effort to develop or implement a coordinated policy, which would inevitably involve priorities and saying "no" to somebody, the program can concentrate its efforts on expedition rather than exclusion and thus maintain a high degree of popularity with all levels of governments. This in turn contributes to the environment of benevolence within which the entire Green Acres Program operates.

Local Matching Grant Stipulations

In New Jersey the commitment of lower levels of government to the acquisition and preservation of open space in the decades before 1960 was uneven and erratic. On the municipal level, happenstances of government philosophy, civic philanthropy, public interest, private recreational opportunity, and a miscellany of other factors determined the extent and characteristics of a municipality's park system. Among the major cities some, like Camden, developed fine park systems; while others, such as Atlantic City and Jersey City, paid less attention to public open space. Among the lesser municipalities the pattern is such a clutter of detail that its description, even in general terms, is impossible.

Among the counties the same unevenness of effort prevailed, although something of a pattern can be distinguished. As counties urbanized, county governments took a progressively more active role in providing open space, usually through the creation of a county park system. Within this general pattern there were those in the vanguard and those who lagged. Essex County, urbanized and suburbanized by the late nineteenth century, had the first county park commission and county park system in the nation in 1896. For a long time the commission was one of the most active, developing urban parks in Newark and more suburban open space in the less intensively developed western and northern parts of the county. In the northeastern part of the state, Hudson, Union, and Passaic—urban counties all—followed the lead of Essex in establishing county park systems in 1903, 1921, and 1926, respectively. Whereas Union County's park system secured large open spaces and connecting corridors in advance of large-scale suburban development, the Hudson and Passaic county park commissions, hamstrung by political machinations, were less successful.[10] In Hudson County the successful development of a county park system was further hampered by a lack of suitable land remaining open, even in the early twentieth century. In 1911, urbanized Camden County established the first county park system in southern New Jersey.

In the 1930s, Atlantic, Gloucester, Cape May, Middlesex, Sussex, and Warren counties established county park commissions; but these, with the exception of that of Cape May County, remained largely inactive through the thirties and the war years. Between the end of World War II and 1960, county-level open space activity increased; and many new county park systems were established, mostly on the metropolitan fringe. Bergen County established a park system in 1947; Morris, Middlesex, and Somerset established theirs in the 1950s.

In the face of this increasing involvement in open space by lower levels of government, the apathetic initial response to the local matching fund seems paradoxical. After all, local governments were being offered free money, and it was being dispensed by a helpful state unit willing to offer advice on site selection and to aid in an application procedure that was not complicated to begin with. The offer certainly looked attractive; yet there were strings attached. Because of the stipulations that accompany the grants and also because of local financial considerations, a Green Acres grant seldom seems an unmixed blessing at the local level. Grant applications are frequently made only after intense local debates and, evidently, with lingering misgivings, for many grant applications are withdrawn before Green Acres officials can act on them.

One grant stipulation is that any tract of open space whose purchase or development is aided by Green Acres money must be open to any state resident.[11] If the local government charges a fee for admission or use of the facilities, the fee must not discriminate against nonlocal New Jersey residents. Another stipulation is that land purchased with Green Acres assistance must remain as public open space; it cannot be sold or traded out of public ownership, and even its reassignment to another public use must have the approval of the state DEP. If a local government accepts a Green Acres grant for an acquisition, it cannot balance its holdings by selling or giving away other open space previously acquired, even if the previous acquisition took place without state assistance. Furthermore, a tract purchased with Green Acres money cannot be used for commercial purposes, even under the auspices of the local government.

A Green Acres grant usually means a considerable financial commitment on the part of the local government. Because Green Acres grants cannot be used for the maintenance of open space, tracts purchased with state assistance must be maintained wholly at local expense. The grants cannot be used to pay for recreational programs, and until 1974 even the purchase of facilities for an open space tract was wholly the financial responsibility of the local government. Green Acres will cover 50 percent of purchase price or half of the appraised value, whichever is lower; so except in those cases when a local government obtains a federal grant for the balance, it must pay for the remainder. When purchase value is higher than appraised value, this remainder can be considerably more than half the purchase costs. Overall, then, the submission of a Green Acres application by the local government involves both immediate and future capital commitment. Because a Green Acres–assisted acquisition means a tract of land that is no longer taxable and will never directly contribute to municipal or county coffers, an application also means a willingness to see the local tax base narrowed.

Neither the benefits nor the costs of Green Acres aid weigh equally on the state's municipalities and counties. The range of local ends toward which state-assisted open space acquisitions can be put also varies from place to place. For different kinds of places—urban, suburban, and rural—the mixture of advantages and disadvantages is very different, as is the net result. Therefore the local view of the worth of a Green Acres matching grant and the consequent willingness to apply for one can vary greatly from place to place. Let me review how different kinds of communities view the Green Acres Program and how they have used it.

The Cities—Extremes of Competence
and Incompetence

The leaders of many of the state's larger, older urban places have seen themselves as particularly ill-served by the local matching program.[12] Their financial condition makes commitment to an expanded park system, even with Green Acres assistance, imprudent if not impossible. But many of the cities possess developed and even elaborate park systems built during the halcyon days of their municipal vigor and financial health. The maintenance of the open space they already have rather than new acquisitions is their biggest concern, and the Green Acres Program cannot help them with it. Moreover, in high-density areas, open space use is high and so is the cost of its development for public use. Until 1974, this meant that in urban areas a Green Acres grant would usually cover a smaller percentage of total open space costs (acquisition plus development) than in exurban areas, where the development costs are usually lower in comparison with acquisition costs.

Because of tax delinquency and the high percentage of tax-exempt land in the state's larger cities, their tax bases are precariously narrow and their tax rates are high. This pales the attractiveness of any action that takes land off tax rolls, even for use as public open space. Furthermore, because the populations of the large cities are static or even shrinking, the local businessmen often think that a tract being considered for public open space could be put to better use as the site of economically stimulating housing or industry. As a merchant in Irvington responded when asked if the city should acquire with the aid of the Green Acres Program the grounds of a defunct amusement park for use as a municipal park, "We need more living space; there is not much more land here which can be developed. Why shouldn't land such as Olympic Park be used for homes or industry?"[13]

Yet for the cities there were still strong advantages to program participation. First, among urban governments there is a widespread commitment to improving residential environments.[14] The Green Acres Program offers to defray considerable expenses in the provision of open space, usually considered an important component of a pleasing urban environment.[15] Second, there are places where open space acquisition does not really involve a trade-off between economic development and tax base on the one hand and life's amenities on the other. Urban municipalities can use Green Acres grants to acquire land that shifting locational advantage has made economically marginal—little-used railroad yards or decaying light industry areas in older sections of the city, for example. Often Green Acres gives the cities the opportunity to acquire derelict tracts still on the tax rolls but deep in arrears and with little potential for an economically productive future. Third, in the cities, open space money can be and has been combined with grants from other sources to attack problems only indirectly related to open space and commonly considered more pressing than any dearth of parks. For example, Green Acres money has been combined with federal housing grants to finance urban renewal and redevelopment projects.[16]

This combination of advantages and disadvantages that the Green Acres Program brings to the cities appears to produce a grant saturation point beyond which the lack of available sites, the erosion of the tax base, and the need to match local resources to those of the state make it unwise to proceed. Where local officials are skilled at using the program, these restraints, rather than any limit of available state money, limit their program participation. As Newark's liaison official with the state on matters of open space put it, "Given the circumstances, we get all the money we want and can handle. We couldn't ask for more."[17] Yet there are cities where this saturation point is never reached.

In most of the state's large cities, responsibility for maintaining public open space and for maintaining contact with the state on open space matters is the domain of full-time employees, often trained planners. Some of the cities, Newark for example, have officials to whom responsibility for obtaining open space aid is clearly assigned and whose knowledge of the program's restraints and procedures approaches that of the Green Acres staff itself. There are other cities, however, where responsibility has become lost in city hall or where it is so fragmented and where procedural knowledge of the program is so low that even agreement on the desirability of open space acquisitions does not get translated into grant applications.[18] Nevertheless, the state's cities have, as a class of municipalities, the highest rates of participation in the Green Acres local matching program. As Table 5 shows, 72 percent of the state's urban municipalities have received local matching grants. This is twice the rate of suburban participation and four times that of rural participation.

The Hesitant Suburbs

In the suburban towns, especially those affluent ones whose populations have large managerial and professional segments, one often

Table 5. Participation among Municipalities in the Green Acres Local Grant Program

	Number of municipalities		Percentage of municipalities	
	In group	*Receiving matching grants*	*Receiving local grants*	*With state-owned open space*
Urban	31	23	72	3
Suburban	315	119	36	6
Rural	221	38	17	24
Total	567	180		

SOURCE: New Jersey Department of Environmental Protection, local matching grant records, 1977.

finds the elite skill pool so important in grassroots environmental politics. Part-time town officials often use their professional skills on behalf of their towns; lawyers, architects, finance professionals, and other experts are frequently available to act in an official advisory capacity or simply to give informal advice. Towns of this sort often operate effectively in obtaining grants and skillfully using Green Acres funds to further municipal goals. Yet there are towns of similar occupational structure, kind of government, and income profile whose awareness of and participation in the program is nil. Perhaps some of the difference lies in purely local considerations growing out of the personalities of the town leaders or the happenstance of their exposure to the program. One important and purely local variable explaining participation appears to be the town clerk, who is often the repository of grant-getting skills in a small suburban town and who frequently watches mayors and councilmen come and go.[19] In these municipalities, ability to take advantage of the program frequently depends on the intelligence of the town clerk or his inclination to serve as an unofficial advisor on such matters to the elected officials.

In suburban places, as in urban ones, the administrative capacity to take advantage of the program varies considerably. Open space is usually a more important matter in suburbia than in urban places, however, because it touches issues of land use and development, issues of central concern in suburban municipalities.[20] Open space is easy to use as an instrument of land-use policy, and state open space aid can be used to purchase tracts that will order development and round out suburban landscapes. Suburban towns apply for grants to purchase open space that has been plotted into subdivision schemes in advance of construction and to acquire the odd-lot remnant after an area had been put into residential use. They also apply for grants to purchase large tracts to serve as the centerpieces of municipal parks systems. The goals public open space can serve in a suburban municipality can be as minor as removal of an eyesore by transforming a neglected vacant lot into a neighborhood park or as major as the preclusion of further housing development by acquiring a large tract being eyed by a subdivider.

In the late 1960s, the number of suburban applications with an ecological rationale increased, reflecting the rise in concern for ecology and the proliferation of local environmental commissions during the period.[21] As the concept of rational land use came to include preserving ecologically sensitive lands in a natural state under public ownership, the Green Acres local program acquired another major focus beyond its almost exclusive concern for recreational open space. Although cities occasionally purchased long-neglected or abused riparian lands for restoration to a natural state, the ecological shift was most pronounced in nonurban areas, where floodplains, areas of steep slopes, and areas perceived as unique in their flora and fauna were often the object of Green Acres local grants.

In practice there is sometimes a very unclear line between using Green Acres money to insure a balanced local landscape and using it simply to thwart development, and DEP commissioners have discouraged grant applications when they thought that line had been passed. Although the most notorious local grant, that to affluent Tenafly to acquire a 274-acre tract slated for residential development, was approved, Fort Lee was informed that a grant request for a tract with potential for high-rise development would not be approved because "the state refused to subsidize residential exclusion."[22] Nevertheless, as already mentioned, many suburban applications have been inspired at least in part by the realization that publicly acquired open space is land safely removed from the path of threatening development.

As useful as open space may be in furthering the goals of suburban municipalities, state-assisted open space acquisitions have stipulations that are especially discouraging drawbacks for suburban municipalities. In view of the way suburbs use public open space to preclude development, it is ironic that fears of out-of-town invaders discourage grant applications. The grant stipulation that a tract purchased with Green Acres money be open to all state residents frequently weighs heavily in deliberations of a suburb considering an application. As Little forcefully puts it, "It is undemocratic, but some suburbanites would just as soon have a pig in their parlour as outlanders in their parks."[23] The matter of simple prejudice aside, many of the inner suburbs are strongly blue-collar or lower-middle class in occupation, and they usually have older populations. They are close to the state's larger cities, and their residents fear the sequence of racial transition and neighborhood decay they see all around them. They fear that a public open space facility might be the germ of such decay. Inevitably when the Green Acres local office receives a serious inquiry from one of these towns regarding a matching grant, the subject is cautiously brought up: What kind of experiences with out-of-towners have other towns had? Have out-of-towners taken over the facility?[24] The same sort of fear exists in the outer suburbs as well. It was cited by the chairman of the Park Committee of the Bergen County Board of Freeholders as a major reason why so few towns of the county, one of the state's most suburbanized and affluent, had taken advantage of the program.[25]

The state's older suburban areas share many of the financial problems of urban areas. Frequently they experience rising municipal expenses coupled with a stagnant tax base. In such circumstances the dedication of permanent open space has an aggravating effect on both sides of the problem, reducing the tax base while committing the municipalities to additional expenses. The budget is also a concern in many of the newer, lower density suburban areas, where public open space for its own sake has a low priority compared to more essential services like roads and sewage treatment. Furthermore, the argument has been made in low-density suburbs that, because there is ample private open space,[26] public open space is superfluous and its purchase and maintenance a needless municipal or county expense.

In suburbia the combination of advantages and disadvantages increased open space brings to a municipality usually combines with participatory politics in such a way as to create a divisive issue. The same town will contain residents for whom the retention of taxable property is of utmost concern and those for whom almost any open space preserved is worth the tax loss involved. For example, a survey found the suburban town of Demarest in Bergen County evenly divided between those who favored selling odd snippets of municipally owned open space and those who opposed it no matter how little used they were.[27] Yet even when there is agreement within a town that a tract should be preserved, controversy can erupt over the use to which it is to be put. A municipal plan to establish an active recreation area on a tract acquired with Green Acres funds in East Brunswick led to a series of charges and countercharges between the town conservation groups and the mayor. Each accused the other of bad faith and of promoting usage that ignored the true needs of the town.[28] Moreover, public dedication of open space, whether assisted by a state grant or not, is likely to be opposed by its prospective neighbors if heavy use is projected. They object to the noise of baseball games and fear the taunts of adolescents and the decline of property values. But less developed open space has its local opponents as well. They fear the vulnerability to vandalism and assault that proximity to difficult-to-supervise space brings.

So suburban towns are usually repositories of conflicting attitudes toward open space, so much so that an acquisition is seldom approved by all and can serve as a point of contention around which antagonistic views on the town's future, finances, and needs can coalesce. This potential for conflict is in itself a drawback to acquisition attempts, for many suburban officials are reluctant to stir up conflict when they can avoid doing so. It is safe to say then that, in suburbia, open space acquisition, especially with the conditions stipulated for state aid, is seldom viewed locally as an unmixed blessing. In some places the benefits outweigh the drawbacks; in some places, not. The result is a 36 percent rate of participation in the local matching program by the suburban municipalities (Table 5), half the participation rate of the cities.

The Reluctance of Rural Governments

The argument that public open space is superfluous runs strong in rural areas of the state. Rural residents have low participation rates in most outdoor recreational activities;[29] and in the northwestern and the southern parts of the state, the local agrarian economy is seen as keeping the landscape open without the need for public open space acquired at government expense. Accordingly most of the counties and townships untouched by suburbanization are little involved in the active provision of open space beyond the opening of largely unmanaged county lands to public hunting and fishing. Rural residents often consider further public involvement in their region unnecessary and provision of other forms of public open space an urban, not a rural, service. In addition, because most state holdings are in rural areas, municipal and county-held open spaces often appear as needless duplication and unnecessary expenses. Acquisitions by township and county park departments in the rural counties have met with strong disapproval springing from such attitudes.[30]

In the Pine Barrens, where title to large areas is beclouded, there is little posting and less restriction of access to privately held property than in the rest of the state. There until recently there has been little concern about open space for local needs, and public dedications of open space have met resistance from the local residents who fear attendant publicity will attract outsiders and increase use to the point of excess. The recent establishment of the national reserve has in some areas of the Pine Barrens only served to sharpen these fears. Furthermore, in the Pine Barrens, as well as in other rural areas, much of the hostility toward state land acquisition in general spills over into a suspicion of local acquisitions that involve state assistance.

Nevertheless, town and county officials in the state's rural areas occasionally manage to convince dubious citizens that the day is coming when land development will close the de facto open spaces now open to them and public open space will be needed. In these places, townships and counties have used state aid to purchase abandoned farmland, riverbanks, and ravines against envisioned future demand for recreational sites. In spite of this, rural participation in the local matching program is the lowest of the three categories, with only 17 percent of the state's rural municipalities taking advantage of the local matching fund (Table 5). Comparing Map 5 with Map 4 reveals a similar pattern. While there are large rural areas of the state where grant receipt has been minimal, urban and suburban areas show up as regions of high program participation.

The Devolution of Responsibility

The two sections of the Green Acres Program thus can be seen to have quite different decision-making and policy-making dynamics. Whereas in the local section the important decisions are made by the myriad local governments who participate in the program, in the state section the administrators of the land-holding units make the key decisions. In one important way, however, decision making in the two sections is similar. In both it has devolved away from its formal policy centers—the commissioner and the advisory committee—and toward those who administer and manage the open space acquired through the program. As a result the key policy-forming decisions in both sections are made to benefit the administrative goals of those who will manage the acquired open spaces. The three major goals of the state's open space administrators are to use open space policy to shape their managerial tasks for expedient discharge, to stay

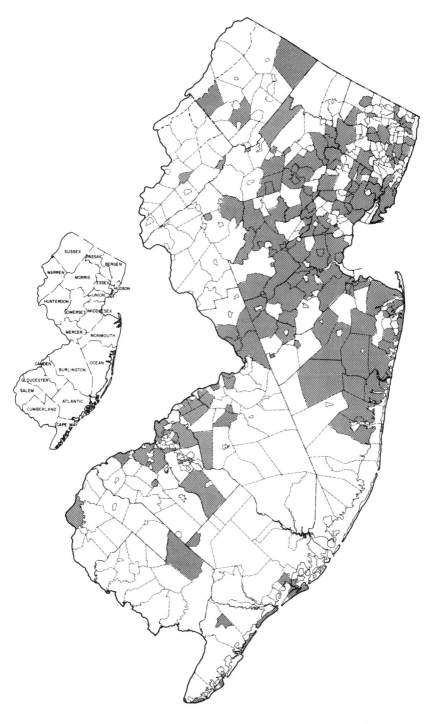

Map 5. Municipalities Receiving Green Acres Matching Grants from 1962 to 1976 (Shaded).

SOURCE: Green Acres Program.

within the general rules of proper bureaucratic behavior as they apply to open space administrators, and to avoid accepting responsibilities that would put them in double binds.

The first goal, expedience, leads open space administrators to favor strongly policies that will define their tasks as simply as possible. It also leads to a preference for bounded, soluble problems, which in turn usually leads to a preference for the routine and the traditional and to the avoidance of new responsibilities with ramifications not fully known. This desire for expedient problems and well-tried solutions expresses itself differently among the various administrative units. For Parks and Forestry it means an adherence to a rather archaic and homogenized view of the good society as family oriented, middle class, and mobile; and it leads to a bureaucratic ideology aimed at providing this society with large, remote open spaces for its weekend and holiday needs. Such open spaces present few problems either in acquisition or in maintenance; their development is relatively uncomplicated and inexpensive; and they attract an easily supervised clientele.

For Fish and Game this expedience goal also leads to a deep conservatism. One of the cardinal points of this conservatism is a strong desire to keep as its primary clientele the state's hunters and fishermen, a group whose demands are known and satisfiable through well-established policies. The opposite facit of this conservatism is a reluctance to accept the new and not yet fully defined tasks of broader ecological management as its responsibility (except on a superficial level). For the administrators of the state's local matching fund, expedience means restricting their handling of grant applications to largely procedural matters, for thus they can quickly process a large number of applications with a small staff. The difficult and time-consuming questions that evaluation on criteria of relative worth and benefit would raise can be avoided. Such a simple definition of responsibility also brings a certain psychic satisfaction; the local program's administrators, who like their work and enjoy their contacts with their clients, seldom have to say no.

The second goal of open space administrators is conformity to the latent rules of public bureaucracies. These rules are usually negative and amorphous. They are not always explicitly expressed, and they do not necessarily come from a specific source. Yet they place very real limits on the range of options among which bureaucrats may choose. Fortunately for New Jersey's open space administrators, these rules are usually consistent with their goal of keeping responsibilities as simple and convenient as possible. Thus the rules reenforce the administrators' predispositions in this direction.

Perhaps the most important of these rules is that bureaucracies not appear to be wasteful. There is always someone anxious to level accusations of overspending and waste at public officials. For Parks and Forestry, acquisitions that conform to the hierarchical model do not arouse such charges. Rural tracts are usually low in per-acre costs; and because they are usually acquired in large parcels, the overhead expenses of purchase are low. Furthermore, the hierarchical model allows the department to concentrate on spectacular natural sites and thereby avoid the possible criticism that it is wasting money on mediocre open spaces. For the administrators of the local matching fund, keeping evaluative procedures to a minimum, and thus being able to process acquisitions rapidly, helps meet demands for bureaucratic efficiency at the same time that it results in internal expedience and in psychic rewards from positive contacts with clients.

Another of these unspoken rules is that an administrator take steps to avoid controversy and negative publicity. Otherwise latent opposition to the administrator's program might be activated, and its supporters might be forced to withdraw their backing. Fish and Game tried to head off public debate over its proper goals by establishing the largely powerless nongame wildlife section. For a land acquisition unit, a swell of public ire over condemnation is an ever-present possibility. By relying on voluntary offerings, usually in rural areas, the land-holding units minimize condemnations, forced evictions, and the negative publicity that accompanies them. Avoiding controversy also means dampening disaffection and debate over the proper use of open space funds earmarked for local governments. By approving virtually all applications, the local matching program discourages the spending policy debate that would inevitably arise among a large group of rejected applicants.

The third major goal of open space administrators is to avoid externally imposed demands that would create double binds by running contrary to the general bureaucratic rules within which they operate or by going against their preference for the known and the simple. Most frequently, these specific demands aim at forcing open space administrators to adopt a more urban-oriented, interventionist policy. These sorts of demands have been strongly resisted by the land-holding units because an interventionist policy would complicate their missions by giving them large, new management problems and a more difficult clientele. Such a policy would also make it more difficult for them to appear efficient and frugal because it would force them into acquisitions with high per-acre costs and needing expensive facilities. Over the life of the Green Acres Program, demands for an interventionist reorientation have come most frequently from the state's planners. Because the planners have never had much leverage in state government and have failed to use what they had, open space administrators have been able to simply ignore them.

This devolution of responsibility to administrators did not take place in a vacuum. Open space decisions are made in an environment of power and influence peopled by those with both formal authority and actual capacity to influence policy to their liking. Moreover, many of those with power and authority would seem to have a vested interest in changing the direction of open space policy. Yet these actors and forces—elected public officials, interest groups, media, and even public opinion—enter into the decision making only infrequently and usually indirectly. They thereby let stand the policy dominance of the land-holding units and the lower level governments. The causes of this passivity, lying in the unique characteristics of open space as a public benefit, in the nature of state-level politics, and in the skills of the state's open space administrators, are the subject of the next chapter.

6

The Political Environment

Bureaucrats are by no means the final repository of power within a state government. They are answerable to the state's elected officials and to its public, both as an electorate and as myriad organized interests. The public and its officials are a source of both general and specific demands to which bureaucrats must be sensitive. Simon, Smithburg, and Thompson emphasize how important it is for a public bureau to maintain the support of those elected officials who exercise formal control over it: "It is clear that an administrative organization must have the support of the legislature or the executive—and usually both—if it is to come into existence and continue to exist."[1] New Jersey's open space administrators have been highly successful in keeping their freedom to use the Green Acres Program as they have seen fit. One reason for this success is that, for various reasons discussed below, most of those within their political environment share the same overriding attitude toward open space matters: inattentiveness. Benign disinterest can be useful as active support.[2] There is a prevailing inclination on the part of the powerful within the state to assume that the Green Acres administrators can take care of open space problems while they turn their attention to what they consider more salient issues. But even when interest in open space is aroused and discontent surfaces, open space administrators have usually managed to avoid the imposition of specific policy demands from without.

The political environment in which the administrators set their goals cannot be dismissed as unimportant, however, and the decision process is not entirely closed to the wishes of those outside the bureaucracy. Downs says of the environment of a bureau, "The persons and agencies affected by the bureau and their relationships to it form its power setting in the external environment."[3] (Although I am dealing here with a decision-making apparatus that transcends bureau boundaries, Downs's notion of a power setting is nevertheless a useful analytic concept that in part guided the course of research presented in this chapter.) The legislature, the governor, and the state's interest groups influence open space policy, occasionally by direct action, but more frequently in indirect, subtle ways. Because each registers its wishes in different ways and has unique strengths and weaknesses vis-à-vis the state bureaucracy, the three are most profitably treated separately.

The Legislature

Although the legislature and the governor share sovereignty, or legal authority, over Green Acres administration,[4] it is the legislature—through enabling legislation, budget control, legislative mandates, and oversight procedures—that has the most formal authority to shape policy to its liking. Although it has used its formal authority infrequently and ineffectively, it has, by what Wamsley and Zald call "tonal" pressure, indirectly exerted an ongoing influence on open space policy.[5]

Two points about the New Jersey legislature must be kept in mind. First, it considers spending to be the most important issue with which it deals. It can become quite histrionic about what it considers waste or profligate spending by state government. Second, it has a reputation for a suburban bias and a record of indifference to urban aid bills.[6] For the land-holding units, one of the rules of political expedience is not to cross the legislature on spending and thereby risk a change in its prevalent attitude of benign neglect toward the program. Although open space programs tend to be immune to the charges of uselessness that fiscal conservatives level at many large government spending programs,[7] they are not immune to charges of waste and inefficiency.[8] The state's open space administrators realize that, should they abandon the hierarchical model of state open space responsibilities, with the nonurban acquisitions it encourages, and shift to the interventionist model that favors urban acquisitions, they would endanger the legislative climate of benign neglect. So because of administrators' sensitivity to the legislature's predisposition the legislature cannot be written off as simply irrelevant. It is usually passive, but even in its passivity it is an important part of the environment in which open space policy is made.

Although its predispositions are an ever-present consideration in open space decisions, active legislative interest is only periodically expressed. It manifests itself at referendum time and then fades into neglect, from which it is only occasionally stirred. Because open space preservation taps public values that make it a safe topic of legislative approval, the legislature has by and large treated the Green Acres Program like motherhood. What Tannenbaum says of the New York State Legislature could apply as well to that of New Jersey: "Conservation— in any and all of its forms—is once again in style; and the assumption of the role of the people's champion, defending the common heritage against the depredations of the "interests," is, in most jurisdictions, a relatively hazard free type of political life insurance."[9] The bill authorizing the first Green Acres bond referendum in 1961 was unanimously approved by the legislature. The second referendum, in 1971, was approved with only one dissenting vote; and the third passed without a nay in 1974, a year in which clouds of taxpayer revolt were visible on the horizon.

In the legislature a small group of senators and assemblymen are closely identified with the program, and it is usually they who initiate Green Acres legislation when it is needed. The most active among them is the assembly minority leader, Thomas Kean, one of the state's prominent Republicans. He sponsored the first two Green Acres bills in the assembly, and the press considers him the program's legislative parent and spokesman.

Once the legislature has approved a bond referendum, there are limits to how much it is willing to oversee the program it has approved. For one, there is an attitude among legislators that their business is passing laws, not getting involved in policy details of the programs they have legislated into being.[10] This attitude complements the practical difficulty of delving deeply into the specifics of administrative decision making or even of understanding any but the most obvious consequences of legislation.[11]

Two factors further inhibit the New Jersey legislature from exercising continual, effective oversight over the Green Acres Program. First, the New Jersey legislature has no standing committees to serve as the external centers of factual analysis and initiative that Redford believes are so necessary for public administration to function.[12] No committees are available to participate in the ongoing, detailed legislator-administrator dialogue that Freeman considers so important in federal-level policy making.[13] Second, because the Green Acres Program has its own funding source outside general revenue appropriations, it is not subjected to the routine program scrutiny that accompanies the annual budget process. Even the few legislators who have taken a special interest in open space do not follow the program closely. For them, just as for the whole legislature, interest peaks when there is a new bond authorization bill on the floor and subsides after its passage. According to a spokesman for Kean, the legislative sponsor of Green Acres, "The program pretty well runs itself."[14]

On only one occasion has the legislature been the source of a systematic review and criticism of state open space acquisition policy. In 1975, the legislature's Division of Program Analysis undertook an analysis of the Green Acres Program to determine if it had adhered to legislative intent and had succeeded in attaining its goals.[15] The report concluded that the state's open space program had an unjustifiable rural acquisition bias that violated the spirit and the letter of the enabling legislation. Two things prompted the legislature to ignore the report. First, because the report did not identify any particular constituencies as being hurt by the program's failings, it did not incite individual legislators to take up the cause of program reform. Second, the report had what Freeman considers a fatal flaw in a public investigation, a failure to convey a sense of impending doom if its recommendations are not followed.[16] Open space is not an area of public policy over which it is easy to work up a sense of doom. Consequently the report and its criticisms were soon forgotten. This lack of reaction illustrates the degree to which the legislature is disinclined to involve itself in open space administration matters, even when its own staff concludes that legislative intent is being thwarted.

The reluctance of the legislature collectively to involve itself in open space policy is matched by a willingness of individual legislators to use their good offices to promote or discourage particular projects at the behest of their constituents. Such behavior is in keeping with the notion that a legislator has a responsibility to look after the special needs of his constituents as well as the more general public weal.[17] On matters of interest only to their constituents, they are limited by the relatively weak power of the legislature vis-à-vis the executive in New Jersey.[18] Usually a legislator can affect a particular project only if he can enlist the support of the governor. Unfortunately for the legislators, the governors, especially Richard Hughes and William Cahill, tended to back their administrators' decisions and had little sympathy for special requests from individual legislators. As a result it is widely believed among state officials involved with the Green Acres Program that, during the terms of these two governors, legislative pressure never initiated or killed a project.

The Governor

The governor is a more active influence on state open space policy. In fact, the legislative initiative for the Green Acres bond bills rests with the governor's office, as it does for most legislation in New Jersey. The timing of the Green Acres bond referenda as well as the statutory rules for the dispersal of the bond fund have been largely decided by the governor. It was Governor Meyner's reversal of his usual opposition to bond spending that launched the first Green Acres bill in 1961.[19]

New Jersey's governors are second only to those of New York in the amount of formal power they inherit when they come to office,[20] and when they take an interest in open space they often get their way. For, example, in 1974, Governor Cahill, following the advice of DEP Commissioner Sullivan, introduced the development proviso into the third Green Acres bond bill. Several of the legislators, including Assemblyman Kean, the sponsor of the previous Green Acres bills, objected. They thought that this was a diversion of funds from more pressing use in land acquisition.[21] Kean introduced a co-opting bill that allocated all funds to acquisitions. The governor made his displeasure known, and Kean's bill died on the assembly floor.

The governor's ability to probe the workings of state government is greater than that of the legislature, for he has a large professional staff at his disposal and he frequently appoints special committees to investigate and make recommendations in areas of special concern to him. As a consequence a governor's interest in public open space can be turned into detailed analyses of programs, thorough evaluations of administrative performance, and an understanding of the ramifications of policy. Furthermore, the governor has been more inclined to follow the recommendations of his staff and commissions on open space matters than the legislature has been.

Finally, the governor appoints the commissioners who head the state government's departments, and these commissioners serve at the governor's pleasure. It is within his power to remove them for any reason and whenever he wishes. Through his choice of the DEP commissioners, the governor is potentially an important determinant of how open space policy will be made, toward what ends it will be directed, and in general what style of administration will prevail in the Green Acres Program.

During the two decades in which the program has been operating, the governor's relationship to it has been woven out of two different threads. One has been a tendency to let the program run itself; to assume that things are going well when no one is loudly complaining; and to turn attention to other, more pressing matters. The second has been the temptation to use open space policy as an instrument in the pursuit of special, high-priority goals.

The governors had good reasons to stay out of open space policy making once the first flush of Green Acres attention and enthusiasm had faded. First, the program's popularity with the media and the general public proved to be extremely robust and rubbed off, free of charge, so to speak, on whatever administration was in power. Why look a gift horse in the mouth? Second, open space acquisition does not require deft, high-level management and executive attention to make things work satisfactorily. Furthermore, a governor has other things·to do. He, like legislators, is most concerned with passing legislation and mending political fences. Sharkansky suggests that governors have in fact very little time left from these chores for contact with their chief bureaucrats on administrative matters.[22] Third, a governor might abide by the Chinese maxim that a good administrator is one who does nothing so that his subordinates have the opportunity to do their best.[23] If a governor involves himself too deeply in the details of policy or program administration, he may weaken the position of his appointees with their subordinates and undermine the smooth workings of the bureaucracy, thus ultimately thwarting rather than furthering his goals. Fourth, because the commissioners are the governor's appointees in the first place, it is likely that they will make every effort to make policy conform to his wishes without his active interest.

For much of the sixties and seventies, executive noninterference predominated in open space policy making. Both Governors Hughes and Cahill had a style of administration that gave much support and freedom of decision to the commissioners, and the commissioners in charge of the Green Acres Program passed this freedom to their subordinates. Decisions were as a result made at a low level, within the land-holding units. Yet once these decisions were made, they were defended by the commissioners and, if need be, by the governors themselves.

Just as the governors had reasons to keep their distance from open space matters, they occasionally had compelling reasons to involve themselves in them. Because Green Acres money was so ample and unrestricted (it could be used to purchase land for any of the broad range of open space uses and even, after 1974, for development), governors were tempted to use it as a resource in pursuing their administrations' most important goals. The fact that the money was outside the general fund and the annual budget made it even more accessible and attractive to them.

New Jersey governors have usually been urban advocates. New Jersey's cities, like so many of the nation's, are incapable of making do on their own fiscal resources and look to the state for assistance. The legislature, reflecting the state' preponderant suburbanization, is reluctant to face up to the magnitude of the problem and the obligations this presents. As a result, initiative for dealing with the cities falls to the governor. When Democrats hold the governor's office, they frequently have debts to pay off to urban political machines or urban-based interests that supported them in the election.[24] New Jersey's strong party system; strong Democratic organizations in its urbanized counties; and powerful, urban-based AFL-CIO further increase this bias.[25] But this urban advocacy has been the case even under Republican administrations, where the assumption of this obligation to the cities is encouraged by the possibility of undercutting urban Democratic majorities. In 1969, Republican Cahill ran for office on a platform that included promises of much aid to the cities. The urban support he drew turned what might have been a narrow race into an overwhelming win.[26] As a result, cities can expect more consideration and sympathy from the governors, be they Republican or Democratic, than they can from the legislature as a whole.

Because of their interest in the cities, the governors tended to see the Green Acres Program as a means of improving the quality of life for urban dwellers and as a means of stimulating urban economies through new jobs and the ripple effects of capital facilities construction. This inclined them to agree with the state planners and urban leaders that the Green Acres state acquisition program, as well as the local matching fund, should be oriented more toward the state's larger cities. In short, the governors frequently have considered an interventionist role the proper one for the state in open space policy. In proposing the second bond issue, Governor Cahill said, "We must have parks closer to the people if this bond issue is to serve all the people. The poor do not enjoy the same mobility as the rich, yet they have a greater need for recreation."[27]

The governor saw to it that the second Green Acres fund included efforts to redirect Green Acres money to the cities.[28] Although municipalities were limited to one funded project and counties to two, this limit was not applied to the state's special aid cities.[29] A priority of open space uses was established for the local program:

1. Land to meet urban stresses and demands.
2. Lands designated open space by comprehensive environmental programs developed at community level by conservation commissions.
3. Lands immediately threatened by development but considered unique or the last remaining area of their kind.
4. Land that would help shape urban development and provide a continuity of open space corridors.[30]

Grants for urban open space received immediate attention as they came into the Green Acres office. The Green Acres staffers helped local officials through the application paper work. Site inspections were carried out quickly, and approval quickly followed in most cases. Within the Green Acres local matching fund, a subfund earmarked for the cities was established. Each of the state's special aid cities was allocated an amount of money proportional to its population and was notified by Green Acres personnel that this money was lying in state coffers, awaiting its pleasure and applications.

The governor's responsibility for weighing the merits of public goals and making the trade-offs necessary in pursuing the most important ones also drew him into open space matters. Once the aura of crisis surrounding the Green Acres Program dissipated, various quarters of state government began to view open space acquisition as dispensable and to consider that perhaps the money could be better spent elsewhere. By the late 1960s, state open space came to be seen as less deserving than other critical capital facilities.[31] The first Green Acres fund was exhausted by 1968; but the governors kept a second bond issue referendum off the ballot for three years, fearing to endanger other, more important, funding of capital facilities by crowding the ballot with a Green Acres referendum.[32]

In 1974, Governor Byrne was again reluctant to offer an open space bond referendum to the voters. The ballot already contained three bond referenda to finance programs aimed at what he considered to be higher priority needs: railroad maintenance and highway and housing construction. He too was afraid the addition of one more bond referendum might endanger those directly useful in combating the state's two major, immediate problems as he saw them, a sluggish economy and high unemployment. When the Green Acres referendum passed while the other three went down to defeat, the governor directed that the Green Acres Program be used in a compensatory manner.[33] He told the commissioner of the DEP to give first priority to projects that would create a large number of construction jobs and have a ripple effect on the state's economy, namely, projects in urban areas, where development costs were the greatest. There are limits, however, to the efficacy of a governor's wishes in the face of a resistant bureaucracy.[34] When a Parks and Forestry administrator was asked what effect this directive had on policy, he replied that it had none; "It was one of those things, a big noise and no follow up."[35]

Barnard writes that a person within a bureaucracy will accept a communication from above as authoritative, and thus as a legitimate source of guidance, only when four conditions prevail: (1) The communication can be understood; (2) the recipient believes it to be consistent with the goals of the organization; (3) he believes it to be compatible with his interests; and (4) he is mentally and physically able to comply with it.[36] Clearly, a communication instructing officials of Parks and Forestry to redirect their efforts toward urban, development-intensive projects would not be perceived as consistent with the best interests of the division and thus would not be seen as a legitimate source of policy-orienting guidance. If not accompanied by some means of enforcing compliance or follow-up, such a directive would be unlikely to be effective. Simon, Smithburg, and Thompson make a similar point.[37]

In summary, the state's elected officials—the governor, just as the legislators—have two modes of behavior toward open space policy. The first is the usual disinterest. Public officials, including a governor with strong formal powers, have limited resources; they cannot attend to everything at once. Usually they face more pressing problems than open space acquisition, so they spend their energies accordingly, leaving the Green Acres Program to run itself. The second mode of behavior is attempts to change open space policy to use the Green Acres Program in the service of their more pressing problems. The legislature usually makes these attempts by mandating priorities in bond-authorizing legislation. The governors, who have more actively sought to change policy, have used both formal and informal means, issuing executive directives and showing special interest in certain projects. With both the legislators and the governor, the former mode—disinterest—has meant tacit support of the hierarchical model. The latter mode has inevitably been accompanied by a preference for intervention. Unfortunately for the legislature and the governor, they cannot vacillate between interest and disinterest and still impose their will on the policy makers. As long as their interest is only periodic, the bureaucracy can usually weather the storm and thwart their wishes until the next palmy era of disinterest.

Interest Groups

One of the reasons elected officials exhibit a disinterested willingness to let policy making devolve on open space administrators is that there is so little pressure from the state's organized interests to involve themselves in this area. Perhaps at first glance this may seem surprising because public open space involves such large government expenditures and because organized special interests and public interest groups have such a great capacity to define public issues. Through publicity and public relations they have the power to create issues or at least to articulate issues that without their activity would remain inchoate and dormant. Furthermore they can choose the context in which they would like a public issue to be examined, and they can impart to it a sense of importance or urgency. They can appeal directly to administrators and legislators and make their views on public questions known much more effectively than can most members of the general public. Willbern suggests that interest groups are especially important at the state level, where "large interest groupings dominate large portions of the political process, and even smaller interest seems better able to exercise control of the particular functional segments in which they are interested."[38] As such, interest groups are potentially important in defining public open space acquisition as a public issue in New Jersey and in shaping open space policy. In fact, they appear to be relatively unimportant.

Most public interest and special interest groups in New Jersey couple general support for state open space acquisition with a lack of knowledge about specific policies or the acquisition patterns that result. Two of New Jersey's large business groups, the New Jersey Merchant's Association and the New Jersey Chamber of Commerce, the latter considered one of the most powerful of all state chambers of commerce, are examples of this pattern of interest.[39] Both organizations favored all four Green Acres bond issues in public statements, but neither follows the program between referenda. The League of Women Voters and the New Jersey Public Interest Research Group have issued statements of support for the program, although they do not follow it closely either.[40] The state AFL-CIO, one of the state's most important organized interests, supports the Green Acres Program because it considers open space acquisition a legitimate object of public expenditure and because the program might create jobs for the members of its constituent unions. Because of the jobs issue, it was especially in favor of the 1974 development clause and lobbied actively for it.[41] Like the other groups, it does not closely watch the program and is little aware of the general thrust, much less the nuances, of state open policy or even whether it is in fact creating jobs.

For the most part the attitude of the state's press parallels that of New Jersey's major organized interests. The *New York Times*, the *Trenton Times*, and the Newark *Star-Ledger*, three of the most influential newspapers in the state, expressed support for the four Green Acres bond referenda in editorials that appeared shortly before election day. All their editorials made the same point: Open land was getting scarce and the little left was getting expensive; therefore the state had to act immediately to preserve sufficient acreage. It would not have the chance to do so later.

Between referenda the press offers its readers a steady diet of articles on state open space acquisitions. The articles are largely factual, usually reporting a just-announced purchase and presenting such specifics as acreage, price, and proposed use. For the most part these articles closely follow DEP press releases and do not entail any independent reporting or critical evaluation either of the acquisition itself or of its policy context. If controversy erupts, however, the press will give it coverage. For example, the papers carried stories about the reputed overpayment by the state for a tract of land in Passaic County and about questionable payments made in connection with land acquired with Green Acres funds in Middlesex County. The *Star-Ledger* carried a major story on the evictions that accompanied state acquisition of Bull Island in the Delaware River, and in it the state was roundly criticized. The *New York Times* carried a prominently placed story about the Green Acres–funded relocation of the Appalachian Trail in northern New Jersey and the displacement of rural families involved.[42]

Occasionally the press has gone beyond stories of particular acquisitions and undertaken critical analyses of program performance. The *New York Times*, the *Newark Evening News*, and the Newark *Star-Ledger* have all run articles matching initial Green Acres goals against accomplishments.[43] In the early days of the program, the *Newark Evening News* ran occasional editorials critical of what it saw as the rural bias of state open space policy. Still, such policy analysis is rare. Aside from Election Day editorials almost all press coverage focuses on discrete acquisitions, usually on the details of the acquisition, less frequently on the controversy surrounding it. Thus the press, although important in keeping the Green Acres Program in the public eye and hence in maintaining its popularity, is like the major organized interests in doing little to exert policy-forming pressure on the program.

In summary, for most interest groups and for the press, public open space acquisition is simply not a salient issue. Most broad-based interest groups approve of the Green Acres Program in principle and support its funding legislation because it fits into their notions of legitimate government concern. Yet they do not follow the program closely enough to have any real opinion of its performance. They are not, then, in a position, nor are they inclined, to direct pointed criticism at it or exert pressure for change. There are several important exceptions to this generalization, however, and the preservation groups stand foremost among them. They have interests and goals that intersect with those of the state's open space policy makers and therefore should be looked at in some detail.

The Preservationists

Citizen initiative in providing open space to the public has long been a tradition in the United States. From the nineteenth century into the early twentieth, providing open space was especially the concern of metropolitan elites, or more exactly, the members of those elites far enough removed from the demands of day-to-day politics and commercial affairs to engage in long-range, visionary planning and disposed and able to back up their visions with private resources when government would not. For example, in the early days of the Palisades Interstate Park Commission, its directors and active members frequently had to beg their peers—Rockefellers, Mellons, or Harrimans—for funds state legislators were unable or reluctant to provide from public coffers. In New Jersey, county park commissions were for a long time after their establishment the special province of the socially prominent.[44]

Today, there is frequent mention of the "preservationists" or "conservationists" in discussions of the politics of open space preservation or land-use planning. These terms commonly refer to those groups organized to promote the preservation of natural (or at least pastoral) landscapes and the conservation of the natural resources of such landscapes. The terms are often used to imply great singleness of purpose and unity of action. Furthermore, the groups subsumed under these terms—the Audubon Society, the National Wildlife Federation, and the Sierra Club, to name three of the most important—are widely considered to be politically potent,[45] with their power ultimately derived from an upper-class and upper-middle-class membership.[46] Although these groups vary considerably in their organization, philosophy of action, and specific interests, there is a certain bond among them growing from their general interests and from a good deal of communication and cross-membership among their executives and more active members.[47]

In several important ways the conservation and preservation groups are similar to the philanthropic wing of the nineteenth-century elites. They have an enlightened sense of self-interest and a sense of responsibility for the public as a whole. To a greater or lesser degree depending on the particular organization, they are interested in public open space and they support an expanded government role in its acquisition. In New Jersey this has translated into their strong support for the Green Acres Program.

Perhaps the most important preservationist group in New Jersey is the New Jersey Conservation Foundation. It has long been active in preservation issues, and its executive director, David Moore, is a highly regarded spokesman for many preservation causes.[48] The foundation strongly supported the Green Acres bond issues, and it alone attempts to follow state open space policy making. Other conservation groups, including the League for Conservation Legislation and the state's various watershed associations, show less direct interest in overall policy and follow it less closely. Not surprisingly, the New Jersey chapter of the Sierra Club has been a strong supporter of the Green Acres Program. Its interest in the preservation of natural areas dates from the founding of the club and remains at the center of its reason for being. When controversy arose over allocating half of the 1974 bond fund to development projects, the Sierra Club, along with the New Jersey Conservation Foundation, supported the allocation proposal even though its primary interest was in the acquisition of natural areas. It thought development funds would most benefit those in greatest need, namely, those in the center cities.

Although the preservationists bear some resemblance to the nineteenth-century metropolitan and national elites in their concern for open space, they lack both the personal resources and the insider's political muscle. A longtime student of New Jersey politics considers the preservationists—and environmental groups in general—politically weak and lacking knowledge of the workings of government.[49] He believes government has assumed many of their goals not because of their political skills but because of fortuitous media and popular interest in these goals. It seems, then, that preservationists support the Green Acres Program because it is in keeping with their general view that only government has the resources to create what they consider a desirable landscape; yet with the exception of the New Jersey Conservation Foundation, they have neither the inclination to delve deeply into government policy nor the capacity to change its direction should they wish to do so.

For their part, the state's open space administrators are both wary of the advice and suggestions of the preservationists and appreciative of their support. The administrators share the view held by much of the public that the preservationists are an elite group articulating and representing the views of society's upper strata. The administrators believe that, although the preservationists deserve to be heard because what they say is intelligent and well meaning, inevitably it will be biased, consciously or not, by their class and status.[50]

The land-holding units are also wary of being too closely identified with the state's preservationists. They balk at suggestions that they should devote more efforts toward the preservation of tracts purely for ecological purposes—tracts with minimal facilties, suitable only for low-density enjoyment. Although located in keeping with their rural acquisition predispositions and arguably of service to the entire state, a large number of such tracts in their systems would expose them to somewhat unfamiliar management problems and narrow their base of public support. Adopting preservation and low-density recreation as a central goal would lay Parks and Forestry open to claims that it had been captured by an elite. Because as already shown, maintaining a stance of impartiality vis-à-vis the state's population is an important corollary of its adherence to the hierarchical model, Parks and Forestry would be reluctant to expose itself to criticisms of partiality toward the state's largely affluent and exurban preservationists, even if by doing so it pleased an articulate and organized interest group.

It should be added that this attitude of the land-holding units began changing at the end of the seventies, and they seem more willing to make ecological considerations an important acquisition criterion. This is probably the result of DEP involvement in managing the Pine Barrens and of the increasingly widespread popular interest in ecological preservation, not the result of direct promptings from preservation groups, of which the land-holding units still remain wary.

Sometimes, however, a situation arises in which the state needs the assistance of the preservation groups. On occasion a land-holding unit wants a tract but because of red tape cannot move fast enough to insure acquisition.[51] When this is the case it may ask a preservation group to purchase the land and will give the group a letter of intent to buy the tract from it when money becomes available. The preservationists make the purchase and eventually turn the parcel over to the state at cost.

State open space administrators consider the New Jersey Conservation Foundation and other groups willing to make such quick purchases for them and providing active, fairly unquestioning support to be valuable policy instruments.[52] Indeed, by changing a couple of nouns, what Dahl said about the relationship between school administrators and PTAs in New Haven could be applied to open space administrators and preservation groups in New Jersey: "In practice, a PTA is usually an instrument of the school administrator. Indeed, an ambitious principal will ordinarily regard an active PTA as an indispensable means to his success. If no PTA exists, he will create one; if one exists he will try to maintain it at a high level of activity."[53] Although they are far from pliant instruments of state policy and conduct their relations with the state with their own ends in mind, one suspects that, if groups like the New Jersey Conservation Foundation and the Sierra Club did not exist, one of the first moves of an astute DEP commissioner would be to create them.

A second exception to the general rule of interest-group indifference are those who believe state open space acquisition works to their particular disadvantage. These include the state's farmers, some elements of its real estate interests, and the sector of the private recreation industry that sees public open space as direct and unfair competition.

Various state farmers' organizations, especially the Cranberry Growers Association, have voiced opposition to the program because of what they viewed as excessive acquisition of working agricultural land. The farmers, through their organizations and the state Department of Agriculture, possess considerable power in state politics.[54] They have forced the Green Acres Program to agree not to condemn working agricultural land and to restrict acquisitions of agricultural land to that which comes on the market without prompting from the state.

Public spirit, or at least the desire for a proper public posture, on the one hand and interest in short-term profit on the other hand seem to tug the land development interests in opposite directions. The New Jersey Builders Association approves of the Green Acres Program in principle; yet it opposes many specific Green Acres acquisitions because they involve tracts the association thinks should more properly be left to private development.[55] The state, in directly acquiring open space, behaves more like a competitor than a regulator of development interests; it is the first among equals. On these terms, the program is acceptable to the development interests in principle and in limited doses. The real opposition of the builders is directed toward state land-use regulation, not the state's occasional out-right acquisition of a tract. Not surprisingly, then, state efforts to control development in the wetlands, and especially the Coastal Areas Facilities Review Act, have roused much more hostility among developers than has the Green Acres Program.[56]

The state's realtors do not seem to have a unified position on the Green Acres Program. Shortly after the program was instituted, the head of the State Association of Realty Boards dismissed it as "a waste of the taxpayer's money."[57] Many realtors, however, like members of the public at large, have preservationist sentiments and act in accordance with them. For example, in Hunterdon County, native realtors frequently inform the county park commission of acquisition opportunities in the offing and occasionally even make special efforts to see that a tract is preserved in public hands.[58]

Finally, there is the New Jersey Campground Association, perhaps the only organized group in the state that implacably opposes the Green Acres Program. This association of those who make their living providing private recreation facilities considers the use of Green Acres money to provide public campgrounds a direct threat to its interests. It has protested to Parks and Forestry and the Green Acres office that such public campgrounds are unfair competition and not in keeping with the venerable U.S. tradition of keeping the government out of what private enterprise does well. The association has little political clout, however, and the Green Acres administrators have little sympathy for it. They find little worth in its arguments, which they consider specious and prompted by little more than selfishness.[59]

Normal and Special Policy Making

The support of both the voting public and most of the state's interest groups assures that state open space acquisition will take place in a largely benign environment. The preservationists see such acquisition as in keeping with their overall goals. Most of the state's influential interest groups consider such acquisition beyond their field of primary interest. This, coupled with the pervasive opinion that open space is a legitimate concern of the state, assures their disinterested benevolence. The potential hostility of groups who see their interests impinged upon by the program is usually restrained by an unwillingness to go against the prevailing opinion of its legitimacy. Taken together, these factors give state open space acquisition a supportive consensus among organized interests.

With this supportive consensus, two alternate open space policy-making processes have evolved within the New Jersey government. They differ in where key decisions are made, which ends are served, and which models of state responsibility are favored. One is equilibratory, or *normal policy making*; the other is *special policy making*. In the normal process, the important decisions are diffused among the state's open space administrators in the land-holding units and among the county and local governments who participate in the local matching fund. The decision making under this process is largely routinized and closed in that it takes place with very little explicit guidance or specific demands from the higher levels of state government or, through them, from special interests. As the term *normal* indicates, this process is in operation most of the time. It is normal, or equilibratory, in that in the absence of unique, anomalous circumstances it prevails. While it prevails, decisions are made largely by fixed formulas. State acquisitions proposals are evaluated against a set of rather technical criteria formulated by the land-holding units of the DEP: Is a tract a good buy? Will it present administrative problems as a unit of the state's open space system? Is it of the necessary high quality for inclusion in the system? These criteria lead the state, without any conscious high-level decisions, into a role conformant with the hierarchical model of open space responsibility. The course of the local matching fund is left to the myriad local decision makers, and the state confines itself largely to pro forma questions.

From the very beginning of the Green Acres Program, initiative in open space matters has rested with the bureaucracy. The prime movers in the establishment of the Green Acres Program were the state's open space administrators. The crest of interest in open space in the early 1960s simply enabled them to convince the state's elected officials that an open space program was needed. The elected officials were approving but passive parties to the establishment of a program aimed at the realization of long-standing agency goals. The formal administrative structure of the Green Acres Program was largely designed by open space administrators and in such a way as to allow policy initiative to diffuse among them.

Since establishment the state's elected officials have for the most part been willing to leave policy making, even in its broad outlines, to the open space administrators. Passing laws is the primary concern of the governor and the legislature. Unless they have a clear sense that something is seriously wrong or that great opportunities are being missed, they are not inclined to look more than superficially at the operation of state agencies. Moreover, most powerful interest groups, having always viewed open space as irrelevant to their principal concerns, have put no pressure on elected public officials to involve themselves deeply in it. This has meant that the administrators are rarely burdened with specific policy demands. They are usually free to establish their program goals to their own advantage and in accordance with the norms and values they bring to policy decisions.

The special policy process takes place when the normal routine is preempted so that the effective choice of goals is taken out of the open space administrators' hands and gathered upward by the state's elected officials. The means to this end can be either formal or informal. The legislature can insist on priority spending either through legislative mandate or by provisions written into an open space spending-authorization bill. The governor can issue an executive order for certain policies to be instituted, or he can press specific projects by giving them special attention. I must emphasize, however, that this second policy process, resting on the articulated will of the legislature and the governor, is the exception rather than the rule. They occasionally get their way, but their expressed wishes do not seep into routinized departmental decision making and thus merge the two decision processes into one. Simon, Smithburg, and Thompson suggest that it takes strong demands from outside an organization to change its preferred policies,[60] demands that if not met will threaten the positions of its members or the organization itself. Such demands are not made on the land-holding units that control the routinized decision process.

Usually, periodic interest and isolated gestures from above are not enough to remove effective decision-making power from a bureaucracy that sees itself inconvenienced by such attention or to change the basic policy goals toward which a bureaucracy orients itself. Unless this higher interest is sustained and accompanied by a willingness to delve deeply into the dynamics of open space administration, it will be ineffective in causing lasting change even if it is embodied in highly specific directives. For example, in 1971, the legislature imposed a priority system on the local matching fund. It gave first priority to grant requests from cities.[61] Yet because there was plenty of money to go around, the matching fund's administrators were not forced to make any exclusionary choices; and aside from some processing delays the priorities caused, the program was not affected by the clearly expressed will of the legislature.

The establishment of Liberty Park, the one major state open space facility in an urban area, was the result of the special policy process, of executive wishes prevailing over bureaucratic ones. Yet bringing the park from plan to fruition required the special attention of three governors over the span of a decade. The overall rural bias of New Jersey's open space holdings in the face of repeated demands by public officials for an urban reorientation of policy shows just how little impact these demands have had in the long run and how much bureaucratic wishes incorporated into normal, routinized decision making have determined open space policy.

There is nothing intrinsically wrong with the normal policy-making process. Although elected officials are the representatives of the people, this does not automatically mean that they should take a more direct hand in determining open space policy.[62] Perhaps they are correct in believing that their attention is almost always more profitably directed elsewhere, toward more pressing matters. Nor is it necessarily wrong that, under the normal policy process, bureaucratic resistance occasionally thwarts the intentions of elected officials. After all, the administrators of the Green Acres Program are experts in open space matters; their elected overseers are not. The administrators can see the ramifications of various policies better, one suspects, than can the legislators. Even a decision-making process that puts great weight on bureaucratic expedience is not to be condemned a priori; for such expedience, when linked to things as frugality and sensitivity to scandal, might be closely linked to the public weal.

It is very tempting, when looking at a policy process in which administrative expedience has figured large, to recommend automatically a greater subordination of policy to the wishes of the state's elected officials. It would be little trouble to construct an argument, buttressed with cited authority, that this would move decision making closer to its proper locus, the people. Yet in this case such a recommendation would be facile and probably not very useful.

First, it may well be that in fact the direction of the Green Acres Program and the course of open space policy actually have been strongly guided by the will of the state's elected public officials. A case can be made for the assertion that these officials send out two sets of signals, an overt and a covert set. The overt one consists of articulated, specific demands for an urban reorientation of policy and a greater voice in its formation. The covert set consists of demands for economy and efficient service. The two sets are contradictory, so making simultaneous and continual demands from both sets on the open space administrators would put them in a classic case of Bateson's double bind.[63] Fortunately, all the demands are not continual; only the latent set is constantly present. It is this constantly present (thereby perhaps more legitimate) set of demands that forms the underpinning of the routinized decision process.

Second, such a shift in the locus of important decision making is probably not possible because it would have to be preceded by a major upward revision of the priority elected officials assign to public open space. This is not very likely in view of the more pressing problems facing these officials and the intrinsic qualities of public open space that make it a wallflower among public issues. Third, such a shift is probably not desirable given the thrust of past attempts to bring open space administrators to heel. If the interventionist-policy advocates had had their way so that great amounts of money had been spent on intensively developed state open space in urban areas, it would have endangered the widespread support of the program.

In sum, the open space administrator and his goals are at the center of the decision process. He is not likely to be removed from this position, nor would I suggest he should be. Now let me turn to the problem of evaluating New Jersey's Green Acres Program and its open space policy as they have been shaped by his decisions.

7

Conclusion

It is often difficult to arrive at any single criterion that is completely satisfactory for judging public policy because public goals are seldom clearly defined and because the limits of public responsibility are usually neither clear nor agreed on. This is especially a problem in evaluating public open space, with the wide and disparate range of public ends an open space program can serve.[1] Open space policy can involve goals as prosaic and concrete as providing neighborhood parks or as ambitious and ambiguous as maintaining ecological integrity or insuring rational land use. This range of possible ends and the tendency of each actor in the process to fit open space into the framework of his own problems (or *issue context*, to use Wildavsky's term) are ever present in open space policy formation.[2] Practical limits on spending mean that all of these public ends cannot be realized simultaneously; thus, any acquisition policy must entail opportunity costs and sacrifice some ends for the attainment of others.

Perhaps the most obvious sacrificed end in New Jersey's Green Acres Program was rational state land-use planning, especially in meeting the needs of major urban areas. But I hesitate to be too harsh on the program for this. Although public open space can be an important element in any comprehensive land-use planning,[3] Healy and Rosenberg have pointed out that public acquisition of open space is not by itself a very effective tool of land-use planning. Not only is not enough government money available to purchase all land that should be open,[3] but open space acquisition by itself can do little to promote the proper development of private land.[4] Thus failure to use the Green Acres Program as a planning tool represents an opportunity lost only if that use was the missing link in a broad, interlocking state effort, which it was not, for there was no such effort.

As Hall points out, the state provided all kinds of public facilities with little thought to the impact of their placement on land development.[5] The state highway department planned with volumes of traffic in mind; it gave no thought to the regional development impact its projects would have. Water and sewer authorities and those responsible for choosing sites for state institutions indulged in the same kind of narrowly focused planning. Although some state officials, notably those in the Department of Community Affairs, tried mightily to gain some state control over land-use planning, they were soundly defeated by legislators fearful of losing local prerogatives.[6] So without effective overall state commitment and without parallel efforts by other state agencies, there was little that the Green Acres Program by itself could do either to further ambitious plans of urban revitalization or to insure orderly development on the metropolitan periphery. Viewed in this light, the failure to use the Green Acres Program as an effective land-use planning instrument was a rather inconsequential failure. The defeat of the planners on the Land Use Committee and their failure to impose their will on the program was a small skirmish in a large war. By itself it meant little; the defeat was more a symptom than a problem.

The ecological ends that open space can serve were, fortunately, more compatible with the resource-oriented recreational ends the land-holding units have vigorously pursued from the first days of the Green Acres Program. The maintenance of ecological integrity broadened the base of support for the policies of the land-holding units, and as such, it became part of their definitions of mission. The program has consequently encouraged rather than hindered the use of open space funds for the pursuit of ecological ends, whatever might have been the ultimate motives of the administrators involved. Through the Green Acres Program some of the state's largest woodland tracts have come into state hands, as have thousands of acres of biologically productive salt marshes along the coast. An assortment of natural biotic communities in which endangered species find suitable habitats have also come into public ownership. It is perhaps legitimate to ask if ecological ends might not have been better served by a program with ecological goals more solidly fixed in the decision criteria with which the land-holding units operated. This is not however exactly the kind of question about opportunity costs I am posing here; and the point remains that the program has served ecological ends, even if only incidentally.

It is the provision of open space for the direct use and benefit of the state's citizens, which has in fact been the main concern of the program's administrators, that warrants the most serious evaluative scrutiny. Unfortunately, the ill-defined limits of public responsibility make such evaluation difficult. To circumvent these problems of limits, I have chosen three criteria. Each has its own advantages, but none is wholly satisfactory. Each has its implicit assumptions about administrative responsibility.

The first criterion is the least demanding of public administrators and narrowly limits their area of responsibility. It asks if there has been a spatially equitable distribution of Green Acres benefits. In other words, have all areas of the state received their fair share of open space? Such a criterion clearly measures what is within the control of those who make open space policy. Yet, as I have pointed out, such an easily quantifiable measure as the location of a public facility is frequently a poor measure of actual benefit delivered to people.[7]

The second criterion goes beyond exclusive concern for the geography of open space provided and into the pattern of use that that geography has engendered. It asks if the Green Acres Program has encouraged a pattern of use in which all segments of the state's population take advantage of the public open space provided for them. This is a more demanding and perhaps less reasonable criterion of judgment because patterns of use have many causes, some of which are beyond the control of open space administrators. Yet it is a better basis of evaluation than the first criterion because it shows benefits actually derived by people more clearly than does a simple geography of facilities provided. The third criterion, based on the specific uses of open space most valued by people, is the most demanding of public administrators, perhaps unreasonably demanding. It asks if the open space provided to the state's population is the kind it most wants and values.

Evaluation on Criteria of Location and Use

Judgment on the first criterion can be quickly made. As I have shown in Chapters 4 and 5, the results of the state's direct acquisition program and those of the local matching program are spatially complementary. While the majority of the state's acquisitions have been in rural areas with a lesser number in low-density suburban areas, cities have the greatest participation rates in the local matching fund. The combined effect, then, has been the provision of open space in rural, suburban, and urban areas. The map of major state acquisitions (Map 1) taken together with the map of municipalities that have received local matching grants (Map 5) show a distribution of open spaces in

Table 6. Use of Open Space by Place of Residence

	Urban	Old suburban	New suburban	Rural
Local parks	45	27	20	10
County parks	19	31	29	27
High Point State Park	8	21	19	20
Stokes State Forest	7	13	17	17

SOURCE: Eagleton Institute of Politics, *New Jersey Poll, No. 7*, May 1973.
NOTE: Figures are percentages of respondents who occasionally use municipal or county open space or who have visited the specific state facility at least once.

which no large areas of the state are strongly underrepresented. So against this purely spatial criterion of distribution, the state has done a good job.

Turning to open space use, the second criterion, public surveys indicate that use rates among the state's urban, suburban, and rural residents are in keeping with a state open space policy that favors the establishment of municipally owned open space in urbanized areas and state open spaces in rural and exurban areas. Table 6 shows the visitation rates at county parks, city parks, and two of the more popular state facilities, High Point State Park and Stokes State Forest. People who live in urban areas disproportionately use open space provided by local government, whereas those in suburban and rural areas place a heavier reliance on state facilities. The pattern of use for open space provided by the intermediate-level county government is an intermediate one, with suburban residents being the greatest users of county park systems.

There are probably several reasons for this participation pattern. First, in urban areas people have less access to automobiles.[8] The condition of public transportation means city dwellers have less access to the state-provided open spaces in remote corners of the state. Second, in most rural areas state facilities are as accessible as local facilities. This prompts people in rural areas to use state facilities for casual outings that would, according to the hierarchical model, take place in municipal open spaces. Travel patterns to the state's rurally located Spruce Run Recreation Area support this contention.[9] Weekend use reflects its status as a major state facility. It draws most of its users from the heavily populated counties to the east: Union, Essex, Middlesex, and Somerset. On weekdays, however, use from these coun-

Table 7. Use of Open Space by Family Income

| | Family income (thousands of dollars per year) | | | | |
	Less than 5	5–10	10–15	15–20	More than 20
Local parks	32	29	29	30	29
County parks	18	32	39	40	40
High Point State Park	21	22	35	48	39
Stokes State Forest	17	24	17	35	31

SOURCE: Eagleton Institute of Politics, *New Jersey Poll, No. 7,* May 1973.
NOTE: Figures are percentages of respondents who occasionally use municipal or county open space or who have visited the specific state facility at least once.

ties falls off sharply while local use remains much more constant. As a consequence, local use becomes preeminent overall. Table 6 shows that county open spaces have an intermediate use pattern. The highest use comes from older, inner suburbs, followed by newer suburbs. The lowest use comes from urban and rural residents.

Although state open space policy has accorded with the hierarchical model, the way the state's population uses open space clearly has not. The hierarchical model assumes that everyone will use locally provided open space frequently and for short visits, whereas spaces provided by progressively higher levels of government will be visited progressively less frequently but for longer periods; but this does not hold true in New Jersey. Urban residents are the most frequent users of use-intensive open space provided by lower levels of government; exurban citizens take greater advantage of the more extensive open space provided by the state and the counties. Furthermore, the use differences show up strongly against variables other than place of residence. Undoubtedly, this is to some extent due to the partial correlations among the variables of income, class, race, and place of residence.

As Table 7 shows, different income groups also exhibit distinct and somewhat complementary open space use patterns. Use of state and county facilities increases with income up to the $15,000–$20,000 per year family income level and then falls off. Use of local facilities is more equal among income groups, though it is highest, but not by much, in the below-$5,000 income range. Looking at self-ascribed class, local parks get higher use from the working class; and county parks and the two sampled state facilities get their highest use from

Table 8. Use of Open Space by Self-ascribed Class

	Middle class	Working class
Local parks	27	32
County parks	39	32
High Point State Park	36	29
Stokes State Forest	28	24

SOURCE: Eagleton Institute of Politics, *New Jersey Poll, No. 7*, May 1973.

NOTE: Figures are percentages of respondents who occasionally use municipal or county open space or who have visited specific state facilities at least once.

those who described themselves as middle class (Table 8). Divergence by race is more extreme (Table 9). The rate of use of local parks by blacks is close to twice that of whites, whereas visits to the two state facilities show a great difference in favor of whites. County open space use rates are more similar for the two races.

The Green Acres Program has, then, engendered complementarity of use as well as geography. There is a rough balance in participation rates, with all segments of the state's population—measured on such admittedly interrelated axes as race, education, and income—taking advantage of open spaces provided by the various levels of government. This evaluative criterion has its shortcomings, however. It ignores the fact that open space encompasses a great variety of physical entities suitable for equally varied activities. It is possible that the widespread use of open space does not result equality of benefits. For some people, the open space available to them might fill deeply felt needs, whereas that provided others might meet only the most casual, superficial ones. My third criterion is based on this point.

Open Space Values

The Eagleton Institute's New Jersey Poll has asked in its periodic public opinion surveys why people value open space.[10] The composite picture that emerges is one in which the commonalities across lines of class, urbanization, income, and race are far more striking than the differences. In one of the polls, people were asked to evaluate the importance of several possible uses of open space. Respondents were to

Table 9. Use of Open Space by Race

	White	Black
Local parks	25	42
County parks	36	25
High Point State Park	35	4
Stokes State Forest	26	2

SOURCE: Eagleton Institute of Politics, *New Jersey Poll, No. 7*, May 1973.

NOTE: Figures are percentages of respondents who occasionally use municipal or county open space or who have visited the specific state facility at least once.

grade each use as either very important to them, moderately important, or not important. Some of the uses—viewing natural scenery and observing the habits of birds and animals—were ones that strongly involve contact with nature. The list of uses also included the more ethereal pleasure of understanding man's place in nature. Other uses were based on escape from high densities and from places dominated by the physical and social accoutrements of human culture. These included breathing fresh air, attaining a feeling of freedom, getting away from people, and finding a place unaltered by man. Finally, there were what might be called more purely recreational or social uses such as running, playing games, picnicking, or having a party, uses not so related to human density or ecological integrity as the others.

Table 10 lists the open space uses about which people were polled and shows what the percentage of respondents in each of four residential categories rated them very important. The differences across categories of residence are small; they exceed 10 percent in only one instance. The most consistently highly valued uses are those that are nature-based or that rely specifically on the absence of cultural artifacts. Both the social uses rank low. Moreover, they are given low ratings by urban as well as exurban respondents. The data give little indication of an urban culture that values open space uses significantly differently from suburban or rural culture.

The importance assigned to open space uses by different income groups (Table 11) creates a more complex pattern than that by residential categories. The overriding message, however, is the same; there is little overall difference across societal groupings. The nature-based and anticulture uses are more highly valued than those less depen-

Table 10. Value of Open Space by Residence

Open space use	Central city	Older suburbs	Newer suburbs	Rural area
Breathe fresh air	80	76	77	76
View natural scenery	64	58	75	77
Enjoy a place unchanged by man	58	57	60	63
Have a feeling of freedom	56	54	55	55
Get away from people	49	43	49	50
Have a picnic or party	50	41	41	43
Watch birds and animals	48	38	40	40
Run and play games	41	36	38	33

SOURCE: Eagleton Institute of Politics, *New Jersey Poll, No. 7*, May 1973.
NOTE: Figures are percentages of respondents who say that a particular use of open space is very important to them.

dent on solitude and contact with nature. The same pattern prevails when importance values are broken down by level of educational attainment (Table 12). Here, however, there is an interesting downturn in the importance of all open space uses at the highest level of educational attainment. For some uses the drop is small, but for others it is dramatic, with importance attached to a place to have a picnic or a party dropping 27 percent from the college-completed category to the graduate school category. Perhaps this reflects the greater importance of career as a source of personal satisfaction for professionals of high educational status. In any case these data also undercut the notion that sensitivity to nature and the more aesthetic uses of open space is exclusively or even especially an attribute of a high-income, educated elite.

It is in the pattern of open space valuation by race—black versus white—that there are important differences (Table 13). Overall, the black respondent group tend to value open space more highly than do the white group, although the valuation differences are not uniform for all uses. The only use the black group rate as decidedly less

Table 11. *Value of Open Space by Income*

	Family income (thousands of dollars per year)				
Open space use	Less than 5	5–10	10–15	15–20	More than 20
Breathe fresh air	74	77	75	69	62
View natural scenery	62	65	66	67	67
Enjoy a place unchanged by man	55	62	63	64	63
Have a feeling of freedom	59	58	57	54	55
Get away from people	34	54	54	53	40
Have a picnic or party	45	50	45	50	46
Watch birds and animals	34	50	42	39	35
Run and play games	29	36	40	36	32

SOURCE: Eagleton Institute of Politics, *New Jersey Poll, No. 7*, May 1973.

NOTE: Figures are percentages of respondents who say that a particular use of open space is very important to them.

important than the white group do is getting away from people. Inversely, the use for which importance rises the most going from the white group to the black group is as a place to have a picnic or a party. Perhaps this grows out of real cultural differences attending racial differences. The idea is appealing because this value change does not show up with the variables that partially correlate with race: urbanization, income, or education.

Nevertheless, the higher values blacks assign to non-nature-based, social open space uses are not accompanied by a decrease in the importance they attribute to what are commonly considered elite uses. Black respondents valued open space for relief from crowding and for the opportunity it can provide to understand man's place in nature more highly than did white respondents. Blacks placed about the same importance as whites on viewing natural scenery and being in a place unchanged by man. In sum, blacks and whites have a similar attachment to what are commonly considered elite open space values.

Table 12. Value of Open Space by Education

Open space use	Eighth grade	Some high school	High school completed	Some college	College completed	Graduate school
Breathe fresh air	76	76	71	72	74	60
View natural scenery	65	64	61	68	68	65
Enjoy a place unchanged by man	53	60	64	66	66	56
Have a feeling of freedom	59	56	52	59	57	48
Get away from people	45	45	47	56	56	45
Have a picnic or party	46	49	44	56	56	29
Watch birds and animals	52	48	36	44	47	40
Run and play games	26	41	37	39	32	27

SOURCE: Eagleton Institute of Politics, *New Jersey Poll*, No. 7, May 1973.

NOTE: Figures are percentages of respondents who say that a particular use of open space is very important to them.

For the blacks, however, the importance of these uses are supplemented by a high valuation of the more social, less nature-dependent uses of open space.

These data point to the overall conclusion that the elite uses of open space are the most valued throughout the state's population. This valuation remains remarkably high and constant among different races, income and education levels, and places of residence. There are, to be sure, variations in sentiment among different social groups, but the variations pale beside the consistencies.[11]

Because these findings run counter to widespread beliefs about open space valuation, they must be defended against some of the more obvious criticisms that might be leveled at them. One criticism might be based on a phenomenon Hennessey points out, namely, that people tend to give the socially proper or respectable answer to a question even if it means lying about what they really think.[12] Thus it could be argued that the respondents gave replies they thought

Table 13. Value of Open Space by Race

Open space use	White	Black
Breathe fresh air	72	82
View natural scenery	64	60
Enjoy a place unchanged by man	62	59
Have a feeling of freedom	54	65
Get away from people	48	44
Have a picnic or party	44	61
Watch birds and animals	48	42
Run and play games	35	42

SOURCE: Eagleton Institute of Politics, *New Jersey Poll*, No. 7, May 1973.

NOTE: Figures are percentages of respondents who say that a particular use of open space is very important to them.

the pollsters wanted to hear or that their replies reflected what they thought they should value, not what they actually did value. The answers, then, would be mere reflections of prevailing norms about open space and ecology rather than evaluations of importance based on personal experience or true feelings.

It is not at all clear, however, that the prevailing norms would lead to low values on places to run, play games, picnic, or have a party and high values on viewing natural scenery, being alone, or watching birds and animals. One set of activities is not universally held to be meritorious while the other is completely disreputable. On the contrary, value messages from the social environment are mixed on both sets of activities. While some people consider the social open space uses relaxing and valuable for mental health and physical well-being, others dismiss them as just so much wasted time.[13] Although nature-based activities are in keeping with the ecological vogue, bird watching and enjoyment of natural scenery do have a certain effete and overrefined image.

Perhaps it could also be argued that the poor and the urban do not know where their true interests lie, that they have been duped by society's value spinners into accepting a set of values purveyed by mass media, a counterfeit set that does not grow out of their own situation or needs. But as Hennessey points out, the capacity of media to change political opinion and values is rather weak. Opinion changes are much more likely to arise from person-to-person contact than exposure to media.[14] It seems safe then to conclude with Lipsitz that, within certain limits, people, including poor people, "can reflect meaningfully on what they expect of government within the context of their own personal problems"[15] and that the expressed preference for access to nature and the solitude and escape it affords grows out of felt personal need and not out of brainwashing or a media blitz.

Perhaps one could take a more positive tack and ask why nature should not be valued highly at the lower socioeconomic levels of society. Elson in fact supplies evidence that historically the more urbanized and less affluent strata of society strongly valued contact with nature.[16] In her discussion of nineteenth-century American attitudes, she noted among the urban poor of the era a great nostalgia for and attachment to remembered or imagined country life and the nature-based rhythms, textures, and social relationships of the nonurban world. For most of those drawn into the expanding urban centers of industrial production and commercial enterprise, the move meant something lost for something gained, and what was lost was missed. For those in less remunerative economic niches, whose meagre incomes and long labor limited their housing options to high-density central locations and reduced their mobility, the loss must have been great. One of William Dean Howells's most endearing characters is Whitwell, a poor rural New Englander. When he was forced by economic vicissitudes to migrate from the farm to the city, only the opportunity to take frequent walks through the odd snippets of undeveloped land on the outer margins of the city made urban life tolerable to him.[17]

As Harvey points out, one of the primary characteristics of modern industrial capitalism is its permanently revolutionary quality.[18] When left to its own unfettered operation, the innovations, obsolescences, advantages, and disadvantages it will produce are, in the main, unpredictable and ever shifting. For those at the margin of society and its economy, the changes seldom bring unmixed good. If change is accompanied by increased material prosperity, the price is frequently high in nonmaterial coinage. For many in contemporary society, historical change has meant, if not material impoverishment, then at least cultural disorientation, loss of status, and threats to self-respect. Such changes might be expected to lead to a defensive revaluation of nature, making it a psychological palliative for painful change. Indeed Morrison argues that just such blows to psyche and status have led to an upward revaluation of nature and thence to ecological activism by members of the middle class who have found their position in society slipping or their occupational mobility blocked.[19]

Williams sees the rise of Western industrial society with its urban focus of economic activity as responsible for bringing "necessary materialism" and "necessary humanity" into conflict. Necessary materialism involves producing or earning those things necessary for a satisfactory material life.[20] Necessary humanity means community membership and a physical environment that is predictable yet malleable. It includes access to privacy and a routine that is sensitive to inner mood and attitude changes. For Williams, the problem of how to have both the fruits of increased productivity and shelter from accompanying unpredictable and dehumanizing changes is central to life in an industrial society.

Those who solved this problem first and most successfully were those who reaped a disproportionate share of society's material output and as a consequence had a disproportionate amount of resources to devote to solving the problem. As Williams puts it, "We can fall back on saying that this is the human condition: the irresolvable choice between a necessary materialism and a necessary humanity. Often we try to resolve it by dividing work and leisure, or society and the individual, or city and country, not only in our minds but in suburbs and garden cities, town houses and country cottages, the week and the weekend. But we then usually find that the directors of the improvements, the captains of the change, have arrived earlier and settled deeper; have made, in fact, a more successful self-division."[21] For the most privileged, the physical part of the solution often involves putting much distance or much privately owned open space between them and the vicissitudes of land-use change. The cultural part may include what Stillman calls rusticating: aping the simpler, humbler lives of other times.[22] It may also include a genuine and active commitment to the preservation of nature.

That the socially and economically privileged are most identified with the preservation movement is often used as an argument for the elite nature of the values that preservation organizations espouse. The argument appears to be specious, for values can be as easily held by those who do not organize under them as by those who do. To hold that appreciation for nature and of the escape from the "necessary materialism" it affords is only important to society's more comfortably placed members is to assume that those who are most exposed to the rough edges of modern industrial society are the least in need of respite from it.

If open space policy is judged against criteria based on expressed open space values, assuming these expressions are valid indicators of true feeling, it is possible to be critical. The findings indicate that neither balanced distribution nor complementary use patterns mean equality of benefits. By providing a set of open spaces that through access and usage link the exurban and the affluent with extensive, nature-oriented open spaces and the urban and less affluent with more intensely developed, high-density open spaces, the state is providing the kind of open space most valued throughout society to society's more privileged strata but not to its less privileged.

So the state's open space policy, as manifested in the tangible accomplishments of the Green Acres Program, must be judged successful by my first two criteria; but the third criterion reveals a real shortcoming. Yet there is a serious question about the reasonableness of this third criterion. Can the state seriously be expected to equalize access to nature by making equal access a goal of open space policy? After all, the inequality is vast, and the state's resources for remedying it are limited. New Jersey can hardly be expected to put a thousand acres of virgin sequoias in downtown Newark.

Open Space, Society, and State Responsibility

Looking just at the results of New Jersey's Green Acres Program and noting the geographic complementarity provided by its two halves and the complementary patterns of open space use it has engendered, one might suspect a powerful central planning entity was responsible for and monitored the program's performance, taking corrective action as necessary to keep it on course. I have shown, however, that this was not the case, that there was no comprehensive oversight. Those who did speak for overall planning and formal, conscious policy making were denied effective access to the policy-making process. Instead, the program was the result of myriad decisions made at different levels of government and largely without regard for other decision makers or the overall performance of the program; there was no one hand on the tiller. The land-holding units, especially Parks and Forestry, made decisions for political expedience and administrative advantage. Legislators, governors, and commissioners also had expedience and advantage in mind when they turned their attention toward and, what was more important, away from open space decisions. Although a happy outcome, it was not due to any forethought of the state that the local grants program worked out to complement state acquisitions. After all, through its refusal to control distribution effectively, the state left results up to unfiltered local initiative.

I hesitate however to ascribe the program results to luck or a number of fortunate yet unconnected accidents and let it go at that. There was a certain connecting logic that seemed to operate through the myriad choices public open space administrators made for expedience and self-interest. Parks and Forestry's moralizing about its responsibilities might have been a way of rationalizing decisions made for internal convenience, but such convenience meant adopting policies that would strike casually interested elected state officials as sensible, proper, and perhaps even just. Parks and Forestry was left alone and allowed to have its way because there was a reasonableness to its courses of action, a reasonableness based on respect for and conformity with certain realities. Policy in keeping with the hierarchical model enabled resources to be stretched, and it courted the support (or at least the indifference) of the politically potent.

In a deep sense, the accomplishments of the local grant section were connected to those of the state section even without any overt coordination between them. Both sections operated in the same land-value geography. For both, the politics and the socioeconomic dynamics of the suburban process supplied the guidelines of practical behavior with regard to the opportunities the Green Acres Program provided. While circumstances growing out of this suburbanizing process gave the state land-holding units the impetus to pursue non-urban acquisition policies, they encouraged the greatest local program participation rates among the cities.

Expedience and sensitivity to the practical seem, like Adam Smith's invisible hand or like benevolent sprites, to have led open space policy makers in the right direction almost in spite of themselves. They have over the sixties and seventies encouraged the state to bring some of New Jersey's most attractive tracts of undisturbed natural land into state ownership. They have led to the provision of resource-oriented county and municipal open space for the exurban and spatially mobile. They have permitted the cities to expand and develop their own space holdings. In other words, they have allowed the program to provide something for everybody. Moreover, they have given state open space policy both a service orientation and a redistributive cast.

For some of the state's citizens, market failure has been overcome and a public benefit has been provided. For others, especially for urban residents, wealth has been downwardly redistributed in the form of grants-in-aid. Looking beyond these positive results, however, both administrative expedience and political reality seem less benevolent, less the creators of fortunate circumstance, and less noble guides for open space administrators.

It is easy to forget what enormous obstacles stand in the way of providing equal access to nature and open space that affords solitude and tranquility. A place for oneself and family on a habitable landscape where peace and tranquility prevail—where there is privacy, a robin on the lawn, and room for children to play off the street—has been at the center of the reward structure of the American economy for a century. This quest has driven the cities outward, segregating them by class and race, and creating the land-value geography of the modern metropolis.[23] It is this suburbanizing process and its ramifications that are ultimately responsible, through the various trains of causal linkage traced above, for the Green Acres Program's results. Whereas it has permitted a geographically equitable distribution of open space, it poses enormous practical problems for those who would provide nature-based open space to those who cannot attain access to it by their own private means.

Because this suburbanizing process is so dominant and pervasive, influencing so much of public life, the barriers it raises to the success of such an endeavor appear everywhere; and most of them are seemingly or unquestionably insurmountable by open space administrators. The purchase of enough open space in the cities to provide for real solitude and intimate contact with nature is simply unthinkable, the artifice of the landscape architect notwithstanding. Land-value geography works against it; the state does not have the money to buy the necessary amounts of expensive urban land. The tax structure works against it; the dedication of such extensive tracts to open space would tear the local tax rolls to shreds without even the small compensation of an economic ripple effect. Urban social ecology works against it; such open space would be uncontrollable by police or citizenry.[24] If the urban-oriented open space schemes of the Division of State and Regional Planning were widely considered impractical, they were models of practicality compared to a policy such as this.

The alternative, equalizing access to nonurban, nature-based open space, seems almost as difficult. Most of the inaccessibility and low participation rates are due to factors over which open space administrators have little control. Indeed some of this inaccessibility and lack of participation is probably due to factors over which the state as a whole has little control. First, the entire trend of deteriorating public transportation runs against such a policy. Open space administrators have little say in matters of public transportation. Beyond running an occasional bus from a major city to a rural state facility, they can do little to equalize access for those without private means of transportation. But beyond this, it appears that mere availability of public transportation is not enough. There are deeper blocks, grounded in the culture and the problems of the urban poor, that prevent them from taking advantage of such open spaces even when the means of getting there are provided. The capacities of park planners to understand, much less surmount, such cultural and psychological causes of underuse are limited.

Practical implementation problems would soon turn into political ones for an agency commited to such equalizing goals. Nothing looks more foolish than programs that absolutely do not work, and policies that run against such powerful trends and deep social realities may lead to just such results. Parks and Forestry found this out when it was persuaded to institute free bus service from downtown Trenton to Washington Crossing State Park. The buses arrived, and nobody showed up to use them. But perhaps the costs of success would be even greater than those of failure. Few of those who now have access to natural public open spaces and who use and enjoy them would look kindly on a policy that compromised their escape into nature and threatened their solitude with the litter, vandalism, and loud radios that would surely accompany increased use of nonurban open space by society's less privileged strata. What, then, are the responsibilities of the state in the face of these problems?

Perhaps above all, open space administrators have a responsibility to understand the socioeconomic facts of life that they cannot change and that impose practical limits on their choices. They must understand that they cannot change the suburban process or the land-value geography with which they must operate. They must also realize that they cannot affect the general trends in public transportation that have increasingly isolated and immobilized urban populations within their cities. Likewise they must face the fact that they cannot do much to help people order their lives so as to be able to take advantage of facilities that are made available to them. New Jersey's open space administrators understand all this. Their policies have cut with the grain of the above verities, not against them, and have lead to the successes of the Green Acres Program.

Administrators must also understand how the above facts of life translate into political constraints through popular opinion and the attitudes of the state's elected officials. As Long says, "Agencies and bureaus are more or less perforce in the business of building, maintaining and increasing their political support."[25] This, Long goes on to say later, "is the necessary precondition for the accomplishment of all other objectives."[26] Political ignorance and consequent blundering could jeopardize the state's commitment to providing public open space. On this point, those who have determined the course of the Green Acres Program cannot be faulted. They have much political acumen and use it to protect the program.

But what if the constraints of social and political reality on the one hand and popular open space values on the other lead to contradictory policies, as is apparently the case here? Two points must be raised. First, as I have shown, these constraints work indirectly through the state's voters and its elected officials. I have used the terms *latent, inchoate*, and *residual* in connection with these constraints. They form an attitudinal background against which open space administrators have some freedom to choose from among actual policies. These constraints do not limit choice to one course of action and exclude all others. Second, although a unit of government must recognize where the limits of the practical and the politic lie, and Banfield argues persuasively that in almost all cases they lie close to current practice,[27] it also has an obligation to work close to those limits and even to press hard against them when need be. One of the functions of government, and state government is no exception, is redress of inequality. Those at different points of the political spectrum disagree on the degree of responsibility, but almost all agree there is one.[28] Redress will inevitably cut against the grain of the socioeconomic processes that created the inequality. In the United States, government in general has less power to do this than in many other countries, but the responsibility is there nevertheless. This is clearly the case for public open space, where a long tradition of rhetoric about democratized access to nature is coupled with great socially and economically determined differences of access.

For the state's open space policy makers the general implications of this are clear, although the specific ones may be less so. They have an obligation to use their knowledge of social and political circumstances to push against the limits of the tolerable in working toward equalizing access to nature and making opportunities for solitude, escape from noise, and contact with fragile living things available to everyone. It does not take much acumen to realize that circumstances will not allow this equalization. Probably, they will not even permit a crude approximation.

The limits of freedom circumstances impose are, nonetheless, wide enough to allow state administrators to do more than they are now doing. They will allow those responsible for public open space to stop thinking of themselves exclusively as land managers and to break out of what Downs terms the *shrinking violet syndrome*, a reluctance to confront new problems.[29] They will allow the state's open space administrators to view themselves more as providers of access to nature, thus putting the current inequality of access squarely in the middle of their problem set. This in turn would encourage them to establish equality-of-use goals for state open spaces and might even encourage them to work toward such goals in innovative and unorthodox ways, for example, by involving themselves in such matters as housing and transportation policy.

Of course such involvements cannot be the main thrust of the efforts of open space administrators. Such a policy would be beyond the boundaries of their freedom of action and would jeopardize the entire public commitment to the Green Acres Program. There are, after all, other legitimate goals for a state open space policy besides social equalization. Still, limited steps toward equalizing access to nature-based open space, both through alliances with those working to equalize overall social opportunities and through their own efforts, seem called for. Who knows, such steps might even gain open space administrators sufficient support to compensate for what they would cost. More important, they would strike a more equitable balance between service to the majority of the state's residents who use and appreciate the state's open spaces and service to the minority who are not in a position to take full advantage of the extensive open spaces provided under current policies. Taken as a group, those who provide open space in New Jersey are a capable and even, within a circumspect definition, an idealistic group. They have the prerequisites to work successfully toward goals that require going against the grain of contemporary society as well as toward those that require going with it.

Notes

1. Introduction

1. U.S. Department of Interior, Bureau of Outdoor Recreation, *Outdoor Recreation Action*, quarterly periodical, various issues, August 1966 et seq.

2. Seymour Martin Lipset, Martin A. Trow, and James S. Coleman, *Union Democracy*, pp. 419–420.

3. U.S. Department of Interior, Bureau of Outdoor Recreation, "State Financial Assistance to Local Governments for Outdoor Recreation and Open Space."

4. Herbert A. Simon, Donald W. Smithburg, and Victor A. Thompson, *Public Administration*, p. 25, make this point: "Many peculiar facts about existing operations-structure, program emphasis, and even staffing become understandable only when their history and the forces that presided at the organization's birth are known."

5. Outdoor Recreation Resources Review Commission, *Final reports*, vols. 1–24 (Washington, D.C.: U.S. Government Printing Office, 1962).

6. Hans Huth, *Nature and the American*; Roderick Nash, *Wilderness and the American Mind*; Richard F. Knapp, "Play for America."

7. Committee on Regional Plan of New York and Its Environs, *Regional Survey*.

8. For a collection of the writings of this group, see Roderick Nash, *The American Environment*.

9. George F. Chadwick, *The Park and the Town*.

10. Ian McHarg, *Design with Nature*; William A. Niering, *Nature in the Metropolis*.

11. K. Lynn, "Neighborhood Commons"; Stuart F. Chapin, Jr., *Urban Land Use Planning*; William H. Whyte, *The Last Landscape*.

12. Ashley Schiff, *Fire and Water*; John Ise, *Our National Park Policy*; Joseph Harry, Richard F. Gale, and John C. Hendee, "Conservation"; Samuel Trask Dana, *Forest and Range Policy*; E. Louise Peffer, *The Closing of the Public Domain*; Jeanne Nienaber and Aaron B. Wildavsky, *The Budgeting and Evaluation of Federal Recreation Programs*.

13. Theodore Lowi, "American Business and Public Policy."

141

14. Elizabeth Tannenbaum, "The Preservation of Open Space in Seven New York Counties"; Ann Louise Strong, *Private Property and the Public Interest*.

15. Linda Grabber, *Wilderness as Sacred Space*.

16. Peter Bachrach and Morton S. Baratz, "Two Faces of Power"; Ira Sharkansky, *The Routines of Politics*; Lowi, "American Business and Public Policy."

17. Max Weber, "Bureaucracy"; Anthony Downs, *Inside Bureaucracy*; Simon, Smithburg, and Thompson, *Public Administration*; Jeffrey L. Pressman and Aaron B. Wildavsky, *Implementation*; Andrew Dunshire, *Implementation in a Bureaucracy*; Frank Levy, Arnold J. Meltsner, and Aaron B. Wildavsky, *Urban Outcomes*; Robert Lineberry, *Equality and Urban Policy*; Bryan D. Jones, "Distributional Considerations in Models of Government Service Provision."

18. Weber, "Bureaucracy."

19. Peter Michael Blau, *The Dynamics of Bureaucracy*; Downs, *Inside Bureaucracy*.

20. Murray Edelman, *The Symbolic Uses of Power*.

21. Grabber, *Wilderness as Sacred Space*; Calvin Stillman, *The Issues in the Storm King Controversy*.

22. Arthur F. Bentley, *The Process of Government*; David B. Truman, *The Governmental Process*; Lowi, "American Business and Public Policy"; Raymond Augustine Bauer, Ithiel deSola Poole, and Lewis Anthony Dexter, *American Business and Public Policy*.

23. Emmette S. Redford, *Ideal and Practice in Public Administration*; J. Leiper Freeman, *The Political Process*; Norton E. Long, "Power and Administration"; Francis E. Rourke, "Variations in Agency Power"; Douglas M. Fox, *The Politics of City and State Bureaucracy*; Thomas R. Dye, "Executive Power and Public Policy in the United States"; J. Lee, "State Legislative Decision-making."

24. Alan Altshuler, *The City Planning Process*; Lineberry, *Equality and Urban Policy*; Levy, Meltsner, and Wildavsky, *Urban Outcomes*.

2. Open Space and the Role of the State

1. Frederick Law Olmsted, *Civilizing American Cities*, pp. 23–33.

2. Tannenbaum, "Preservation of Open Space," p. 10.

3. August Heckscher, *Open Spaces*, pp. 195–215.

4. Ruth Miller Elson, *Guardians of Tradition*, pp. 15–40.

5. Olmsted, *Civilizing American Cities*, p. 70.

6. Knapp, "Play for America."

7. Lee Franklin Hanmer, *Public Recreation, Park, Playgrounds and Outdoor Recreation Facilities*, pp. 40–41.

8. Olmsted, *Civilizing American Cities*, p. 105.

9. Outdoor Recreation Resources Review Commission, *Outdoor Recreation for America*, pp. 14–16.

10. Chadwick, *Park and the Town*, p. 80.

11. Elson, *Guardians of Tradition*.

12. George Catlin, "An Artist Proposes a National Park," p. 5.

13. Frederick Law Olmsted, "The Value and Care of Parks."

14. Ibid., p. 22.

15. Outdoor Recreation Resources Review Commission, *Outdoor Recreation Literature*, p. 120.

16. For a more detailed discussion of federal conservation efforts during this period, see Henry Clepper, *Origins of American Conservation*.

17. Henry Clepper treats the nineteenth-century origins of state forests and state forestry in his *Professional Forestry in the United States*, pp. 82–101.

18. Frank Graham, Jr., *The Adirondack Park*, pp. 119–132.

19. Outdoor Recreation Resources Review Commission, *Outdoor Recreation Literature*, p. 122.

20. Marion Clawson and Jack L. Knetsch, *Economics of Outdoor Recreation*, p. 38.

21. Ibid.

22. Marion Clawson, R. Burnell Held, and C. H. Stoddard, *Land for the Future*, table 20, p. 136.

23. See Clayne R. Jensen, *Outdoor Recreation in America*, p. 57–96, for a more detailed discussion of the open space assistance various federal agencies give to state and local governments.

24. In 1978, the Bureau of Outdoor Recreation was reorganized, given additional responsibility for running the federal government's local aid programs in conservation and historic preservation, and renamed the Heritage, Conservation and Recreation Service.

25. See Raymond O'Brien, "The Role of Highland Aesthetics in the Creation of an Interstate Park."

26. Tannenbaum, "Preservation of Open Space," p. 164.

27. Morton Grodzins, "The Many American Governments and Outdoor Recreation," p. 67.

28. Ibid.

29. Tannenbaum, "Preservation of Open Space," p. 283.

30. Heckscher, *Open Spaces*, p. 9; Diana R. Dunn, "Leisure Resources in America's Inner Cities"; Charles E. Little, "Preservation Policy and Personal Perception," p. 52.

31. Daniel J. Elazar, "The States and the Nation," p. 449; York Willbern, "The States as Components in an Areal Division of Power," p. 72.

32. Willbern, "States as Components," p. 87.

33. James R. O'Connor, *The Fiscal Crisis of the State*, pp. 130–133.

34. Willbern, "States as Components," p. 84.

35. Alan K. Campbell and Donna E. Shalala, "Problems Unsolved, Solutions Untried," pp. 24–26.

36. Council of State Governments, *State Responsibility in Urban Regional Development*.

37. Chapin, *Urban Land Use Planning*, p. 420.

38. Campbell and Shalala, "Problems Unsolved, Solutions Untried," pp. 4–26.

3. The Origins of the Green Acres Program

1. Simon, Smithburg, and Thompson, *Public Administration*, p. 31.
2. Dunshire, *Implementation in a Bureaucracy*.
3. New Jersey State Planning Board, *Parks and Public Lands in New Jersey*.
4. Tannenbaum, "Preservation of Open Space," p. 178.
5. Regional Plan Association, *The Race for Open Space*, p. 67.
6. Committee on Regional Plan of New York and Its Environs, *Regional Plan of New York and Its Environs*.
7. Hanmer, *Public Recreation*, p. 142.
8. Robert A. Caro, *The Power Broker*, pp. 308–310.
9. New Jersey State Planning Board, *Parks and Public Lands*, p. 6.
10. Ibid., p. 7.
11. New Jersey Department of Conservation and Economic Development, Bureau of State and Regional Planning, *Development Plan for New Jersey*.
12. Ibid., p. 31.
13. Budd Chavooshian, former Director, New Jersey Division of State and Regional Planning, related in an interview a story that illustrates the tradition of extreme parsimony within the New Jersey state government and the differences this created between New Jersey's open space planning and that of its emulated neighbor, New York. When New Jersey acquired Island Beach, a long barrier island similar to that on which Robert Moses had created the Jones Beach facilities, New Jersey's Commissioner of Conservation and Economic Development (Salvatore Bontempo) invited Moses over to New Jersey to look at the beach and make suggestions for its development. Together the commissioner and Moses walked the dunes, and soon Moses's plan took shape—causeways would go here, grand bathhouses with pennants fluttering in the salty breeze would go there. With some hesitation the commissioner asked how much this would cost, and when Moses replied that with luck and cost cutting it should not total more than $75 million, the commissioner almost fell over. He knew he might as well ask for the moon; such an amount was unthinkable in New Jersey. Eventually a much more modest development plan, one costing a small fraction of Moses's "economical" estimate, was settled on.
14. Guy Benveniste, *The Politics of Expertise*, pp. 1–21, discusses many of the reasons for this lack of connection between those who make long-range plans and those who actually set policy. See also Simon, Smithburg, and Thompson, *Public Administration*, pp. 423–450. On p. 445, while addressing the frequent disjunction between planning goals and the means of implementation available to planners, they suggest (perhaps wryly) that a "governmental agency that is entrusted with a goal and with very few and ineffective means for achieving that goal is likely to be called a planning agency."
15. Martin L. Needleman and Carolyn Emerson Needleman, *Guerrillas in the Bureaucracy*, pp. 48–50.
16. Donald Stansfield, interview.
17. Ann Slatterthwaite and George T. Marcou, "Planning Open Space."

18. See, for example, Council of State Governments, *State Responsibility*, or Regional Plan Association, *Race for Open Space*.

19. Arthur Hawthorne Carhart, "Historical Development of Outdoor Recreation," p. 120.

20. See Elmo Richardson, *Dams, Parks and Politics*, chaps. 7–10, for a detailed discussion of the Echo Park controversy.

21. Outdoor Recreation Resources Review Commission, *Outdoor Recreation for America*, p. 2.

22. Their studies culminated in 1962 with the release of *Spread City*.

23. Jean Gottmann, *Megalopolis*.

24. Council of State Governments, *State Responsibility*, p. 148.

25. Ibid., p. 147.

26. Ibid., p. 148.

27. Some of the other state reports with similar conclusions were Massachusetts Department of Natural Resources, *Making Massachusetts a Better Place to Live, Work and Play*; State of California, *California Public Outdoor Recreation Plan*; Minnesota Department of Conservation, *Land, Land Use and Recreation*.

28. New York Conservation Law, Article 16-C, 879.

29. New Jersey Department of Conservation and Economic Development, *The Need for a State Recreational Land Acquisition and Development Program*, p. viii, n. 2.

30. Stansfield, interview.

31. Chavooshian, interview.

32. Ibid.

33. New Jersey Department of Conservation and Economic Development, *Report on Land Use Planning*, p. 22.

34. Chavooshian, interview.

35. New Jersey Department of Conservation and Economic Development, *Acquisition and Development Program*.

36. Ibid.

37. Stansfield, interview.

38. Chavooshian, interview; Downs, *Inside Bureaucracy*, p. 5.

39. Bauer, Pool, and Dexter, *American Business and Public Policy*, discuss the importance of prevailing sentiment in determining the position of interest groups on issues.

40. New Jersey Department of Environmental Protection, *Establishing Green Belts and Parks*.

41. Bonds "Yes" Committee, Green Acres promotional packet, undated (1961).

42. Willbern, "States as Components," p. 86.

43. In 1961, the vote was 742,396 in favor, 507,897 against; in 1971, 1,079,200 in favor, 512,985 against; in 1974, 1,000,385 in favor, 816,919 against; in 1978, 880,306 in favor, 694,197 against.

44. James G. March and Herbert A. Simon, *Organizations*, p. 150.

45. The Division of Water Resources is the state's third major land-holding unit. It has been involved with the Green Acres Program peripherally. Reser-

voir construction was one of the uses for which money from the first Green Acres fund could be used, although there was no strong logical or functional connection between open space preservation and reservoir construction. In the early 1960s, all the state's land-holding divisions, including Water Resources, were under the commissioner of the DCED. Thus it was convenient for him to take advantage of the cresting popular and government interest in open space preservation and graft reservoir construction on the Green Acres Program. This arrangement ended in 1969 with the passage of a separate water resources bond referendum, and money for reservoir construction no longer came out of the Green Acres fund. More recently, the Division of Water Resources has opened some of its facilities to public recreation and jointly administered with the Division of Parks and Forestry two reservoir-recreation complexes, those at Spruce Run and Round Valley. Yet, open space as it is here considered has never been of more than minimal concern to the division. Although the division is represented on the Land Use Committee, it has not been an active party in formulation of open space policy.

46. Chavooshian, interview.

47. Richard Sullivan, interview.

48. Between 1962 and 1975, New Jersey received a total of $44.1 million in federal open space acquisition aid from both the Department of Housing and Urban Development and the BOR. Of the total, $19.3 million was used for state acquisitions, and $22.7 million was channeled through the state to local governments. New Jersey Department of Environmental Protection, various internal documents.

49. New Jersey Department of Environmental Protection, *Administrative Order No. 15.*

50. Sullivan, interview.

4. State Acquisition Policy

1. John Kraml, interview.

2. In the early and mid-1960s, both the *Star-Ledger* and the *Newark Evening News* ran articles critical of the slow acquisition rate. The *Star-Ledger*'s October 29, 1966, article, "Hit or Miss Appraisals Stall Land Buying," was typical of the genre in its criticism of the state for its inability to move quickly to acquire open space.

3. Sullivan, interview.

4. Queale and Lynch, Inc., "Urban State Parks Study," p. 6.

5. Ibid.

6. Arthur Blumenthal, interview.

7. Such behavior should not be viewed as uncommon. Albert O. Hirschman, *Exit, Voice and Loyalty*, pp. 55–61, observes that organizations often strive to establish and support other organizations—ostensibly competitors—that will relieve them of unwanted responsibility.

8. John Blydenburgh, "Party Organizations," pp. 110–137.

9. Aaron B. Wildavsky, "The Agency, Roles and Perspectives," p. 69, makes a similar point: "If a department head or budget officer is concerned only with maximizing appropriations that is one thing, but if he has other goals—strong policy preferences, etc.—then a simple maximizing position will not be appropriate."

10. New Jersey Department of Environmental Protection, Division of Parks, Forestry and Recreation, *New Jersey Open Space Recreation Plan*.

11. Downs, *Inside Bureaucracy*, p. 237, defines *bureaucratic ideology* as an "image of that portion of the good society relevant to the functions of the particular bureau concerned, plus the chief means of constructing that portion." This is exactly how the term is used here.

12. Elizabeth H. Haskill and Victoria S. Price, *State Environmental Management*, p. 123.

13. The Advisory Fish and Game Council regulates game seasons, bag limits, and the methods of taking game. It also appoints the director of Fish and Game (with the approval of the governor). The eleven members are appointed by the governor: six recommended by the state Federation of Sportsmen's Clubs, three by the state Agricultural Convention, and two by the commercial fishing industry.

14. Gary L. Wamsley and Mayer W. Zald, *The Political Economy of Public Organizations*, p. 42.

15. Mitchell Smith, interview.

16. Ibid.

17. David Moore, interview.

18. Philip H. Burch, Jr., "Interest Groups," pp. 95–96.

19. Smith, interview.

20. Downs, *Inside Bureaucracy*, p. 242, suggests that a bureau will adopt an ideology of service to society as a whole, even if its actual base of support is a small client group, because by doing so it obscures its actual schedule of delivered, tangible benefits to its small group of clients.

21. Indeed, such a shift in goals would probably gain Fish and Game little while involving considerable political costs. As Rourke, "Variations in Agency Power," p. 243, writes, "A small clientele that is highly self conscious and dedicated to the pursuit of certain tangible objectives which it shares with the agency can in the last analysis be much more helpful than a large clientele which has neither of these characteristics."

22. New Jersey of Department of Conservation and Economic Development, Bureau of State and Regional Planning, *Development Plan for New Jersey*.

23. For an entertaining description and history of the Pine Barrens up to and including the jetport proposal, see John McPhee, *The Pine Barrens*.

24. Two important pieces of research on the region, Jack McCormick, *The Pine Barrens*, and Jack McCormick and Leslie Jones, *The Pine Barrens*, were the result of studies sponsored by the National Park Service. Both have served widely as models of regional ecological studies.

25. David Fairbrothers, interview. The reserve was established as part

of an omnibus parks bill, the National Parks and Recreation Act of 1978 (PL 95-625).

26. *Congressional Record*, October 12, 1978, pp. 18517–18519.

27. Robert Marshall, interview.

28. Ibid.

29. Ibid.

30. Governor's Pinelands Review Committee, *Planning and Management of the New Jersey Pinelands*.

31. New Jersey Pinelands Commission, *Draft Comprehensive Management Plan*.

32. Marshall, interview.

33. Ibid.

34. Three of the most important were: New Jersey State Planning Board, *Parks and Public Lands*; idem, *Where Shall We Play?*; New Jersey Department of Conservation and Economic Development, Bureau of State and Regional Planning, *Development Plan for New Jersey*.

35. Stansfield, interview.

36. League of Women Voters, *New Jersey*, p. 164.

37. Simon, Smithburg, and Thompson, *Public Administration*, p. 446, believe there is an intrinsic point of conflict between planners, concerned primarily with long-term goals, and administrators, charged with day-to-day operations. The three suggest that administrators tend to resist the intrusion of planners into their area of operation, even if it can be demonstrated that what the planners propose will have long-term benefits.

38. Melvin M. Webber, "Comprehensive Planning and Social Responsibility," p. 238, states that "the city planner's realistic idealism, his orientation toward the whole city, and his focus upon future conditions have placed him in a position of intellectual leadership." Though this may or may not have been the case, the statement does indicate that such self-important notions were abroad in the planning profession and would have served to reinforce the planners' belief that they had a right to a strong voice in the Green Acres Program.

39. Stansfield, interview.

40. See Dunshire, *Implementation in a Bureaucracy*, p. 221, for a discussion of the relationship between a person's position in a bureaucratic hierarchy and the degree of legitimacy that person's communications will be accorded by their recipients.

41. March and Simon, *Organizations*, p. 129, suggest that persuasion will be effective only when agencies have "common deep-level goals." Planning assumed this to be the case, but clearly it was not; hence perhaps the ineffectiveness of this approach.

42. Stansfield, interview.

43. Louis Nagy, interview.

44. Downs, *Inside Bureaucracy*, p. 218, defines *supermen planners* as those who "develop far more original, daring, sweeping, and internally consistent

visions of what should be done than if they actually had to deal with the disenchanting welter of conflicting interests in the real world."

45. John N. Kolesar, "The States and Urban Planning and Development," p. 117.

46. Stansfield, interview.

47. According to Norman Beckman, "The Planner as a Bureaucrat," p. 262, the planners commit a cardinal error of their profession by allowing themselves to acquire such an image: "Planners above all cannot afford to be called dreamers or ivory tower types. To put out proposals that clearly have little chance of acceptance or accomplishment inevitably reduces a planner's always limited supply of public confidence and makes acceptance of subsequent proposals less likely, regardless of their merit."

48. Freeman, *Political Process*, p. 71; Chavooshian, interview.

49. League of Women Voters, *New Jersey*, p. 169.

50. Stansfield, interview.

51. Simon, Smithburg, and Thompson, *Public Administration*, p. 447, suggest that organizational distance between planners and administrators can work to the advantage of administrators who wish to ignore suggestions for change advanced by planners.

52. Thomas Hall, *Land Use Planning and Management, The Role of State Government*, pp. 99–101.

53. Downs, *Inside Bureaucracy*, pp. 212–225, gives a detailed treatment of bureaucratic territoriality and the problems that can arise when an agency believes its "policy space" has been invaded by another agency.

54. Graham T. Allison, "Bureaucratic Politics," p. 228.

55. Orville F. Poland, "Planning as a Function of Public Administration and Evaluation."

56. Robert Stokes, interview.

57. Needleman and Needleman, *Guerrillas in the Bureaucracy*, p. 254. In 1980 the DEP was reorganized to place administrative responsibility for the Green Acres Program within the Division of Parks and Forestry, which was renamed the Division of Parks, Forestry and Green Acres. This reorganization confirms (and perhaps legitimizes) the long-term dominance of the program by the state's open space managers.

58. March and Simon, *Organizations*, p. 150.

59. Sullivan, interview. Although a claim such as Sullivan's may be self-serving, it was widely corroborated by others involved with the Green Acres Program during his term as commissioner.

60. Ibid.

61. Chavooshian, interview.

62. Freeman, *Political Process*, p. 69, uses the term *strategic sensitivity* specifically to refer to a bureau leader's ability to anticipate the responses to his bureau's actions by a legislative committee and to behave accordingly. By extension the term can be used more generally to describe sensitivity to any inchoate and latent but potent demands in the administrator's environment, de-

mands that can be turned into specific, inconvenient ones by the actions of politically unskilled administrators.

63. Downs, *Inside Bureaucracy*, pp. 134–136, presents a general, theoretical exposition of authority leakage in a bureaucracy.

64. Nagy, interview.

65. Kraml, interview.

66. Fox, *City and State Bureaucracy*, p. 21.

67. Nagy, interview.

68. Smith, interview.

69. Sharkansky, *Routines of Politics*, p. 251.

70. Michel Crozier, *The Bureaucratic Phenomenon*, p. 81.

71. Downs, *Inside Bureaucracy*, p. 78, suggests that "each official will vary in the degree to which he complies with directives from his superiors, depending on whether these directives favor or oppose his own interest. Subordinates will zealously expedite some orders, carry out others with only mild enthusiasm, drag their feet seriously on still others, and completely ignore a few, and it is almost impossible for superiors to avoid this outcome." Simon, Smithburg, and Thompson, *Public Administration*, p. 393, suggest that bureaucratic inertia unrelated to any objective evaluation of the consequences of a new type of action may in some instances be responsible for resistance to demands for that action. According to these authors, inertia is "due to the painfulness of altering habitual and accustomed ways of doing things." For Parks and Forestry, the development of Liberty Park was certainly not in keeping with its habitual or accustomed ways.

72. Stansfield, interview.

73. The correlation coefficient (Pearson's product moment correlation) is a measure of association with an upper limit of 1 (+ or −) for a perfect association and a lower limit of 0 for no associative relationship. For the formula and a discussion of the statistic, see Hubert M. Blalock, Jr., *Social Statistics*, pp. 376–383.

74. New Jersey Department of Community Affairs, Division of State and Regional Planning, *New Jersey Municipal Profiles*. The division's scheme has eight categories, making it overly complex for my purposes of analysis, so I have combined the eight categories into three in the following manner:

Urban center Urban center–rural	Urban
Suburban-urban Suburban Suburban-rural	Suburban
Rural Rural center Rural center–rural	Rural

75. New Jersey State Legislature, Office of Fiscal Affairs, *The New Jersey Green Acres Land Acquisition Program*.

5. The Local Matching Fund

1. Twenty million dollars, a third of the money raised by the first bond issue, was allocated to the local matching fund. Forty million and one hundred million dollars—half of the second and third bond issues, respectively—went into the local fund. Although, among the states, the amount of money New Jersey makes available to its local governments through the Green Acres local matching fund is unusual, its financial assistance to lower levels of government for open space acquisition is by no means unique. In fact this kind of assistance is usually a concomitant of an active state program of direct land acquisition; and in 1976, twenty-two states had such assistance programs in operation. Most programs were like that of New Jersey in that spending initiative rested with local governments. Counties and municipalities would apply for state funds, detailing the specific projects toward which state money was to be applied. The state would then evaluate the requests and, if it approved of the project, make a grant for part, and in rare cases for all, of the total costs. U.S. Department of Interior, Bureau of Outdoor Recreation, "State Financial Assistance."

2. Howard Wolf, interview.

3. Edward Beardsley, interview.

4. Wolf, interview.

5. Weber, "Bureaucracy."

6. Beardsley, interview.

7. Blau, *Dynamics of Bureaucracy*, p. 242.

8. Simon, Smithburg, and Thompson, *Public Administration*, p. 117.

9. Blumenthal, interview.

10. Hanmer, *Public Recreation*, pp. 43–44.

11. This and the following stipulations are from the New Jersey Department of Environmental Protection, "General Policy Statements."

12. Wolf, interview.

13. "Green Acres Aid Pledged to Cities," *New York Times*, November 15, 1971.

14. Morris J. Levitt and Eleanor G. Feldbaum, *State and Local Government and Politics*, p. 274.

15. Garrett Eckbo, *Public Landscape*, pp. 16–36; Heckscher, *Open Spaces*, pp. 243–349.

16. Wolf, interview.

17. Blumenthal, interview.

18. Beardsley, interview.

19. Wolf, interview.

20. Whyte, *Last Landscape*, is perhaps the most important and widely cited source on the relationship between preserved open spaces and suburban-exurban land development.

21. Wolf, interview.

22. Sullivan, interview.

23. Charles E. Little, *The Challenge of Land*, p. 28.

24. Beardsley, interview.

25. "Only 5 Bergen Municipalities Seek State's Open Space Funds," *New York Times*, November 25, 1963.

26. Arthur B. Gallion and Simon Eisner, *The Urban Pattern*, p. 255.

27. Little, *Challenge of Land*, p. 74.

28. "Garden Club Circulates Anti-park Petition in East Brunswick," *Home News*, October 10, 1976.

29. Eva Mueller and Gerald Gurin, *Participation in Outdoor Recreation*, p. 61.

30. Barry Lock, interview.

6. The Political Environment

1. Simon, Smithburg, and Thompson, *Public Administration*, p. 383.

2. See Fox, *City and State Bureaucracy*, especially chap. 1, for a discussion of the strengths of and restraints on public service bureaucracies in their dealings with elected public officials.

3. Downs, *Inside Bureaucracy*, p. 44.

4. Gordon Tullock, *Politics of Bureaucracy*, pp. 51–63, uses the term *sovereignty* to indicate the ultimate legal authority over the actions of a bureaucracy, as distinct from the administrative authority of a superior.

5. Wamsley and Zald, *Political Economy*, p. 27.

6. Wayne L. Francis, *Legislative Issues in the Fifty States*, p. 39, discusses legislative priorities; A. James Reichley, "The Political Containment of Cities," p. 189, deals with the biases of state legislatures.

7. Nienaber and Wildavsky, *Budgeting and Evaluation*, p. 84.

8. Long, "Power and Administration," p. 11, suggests that "economy and efficiency are the two objectives a laissez-faire society can prescribe in peacetime as over-all government objectives." If this is the case, these objectives will be a source of residual, latent demands in the environment of an agency, demands that may sometimes be overridden by the pursuit of other goals and that may sometimes emerge as the primary consideration in agency decision making.

9. Tannenbaum, "Preservation of Open Space," p. 282.

10. Levitt and Feldbaum, *State and Local Government*, p. 318.

11. Ibid., p. 236.

12. Redford, *Ideal and Practice*, p. 100.

13. Freeman, *Political Process*, pp. 96–115.

14. Jane Burgio, interview.

15. New Jersey State Legislature, Office of Fiscal Affairs, *Land Acquisition Program*.

16. Freeman, *Political Process*, p. 104.

17. Levitt and Feldbaum, *State and Local Government*, p. 244.

18. Alan Rosenthal, "The Governor, the Legislature and State Policy Making."

19. Chavooshian, interview.

20. Thad L. Beyle, "The Governor's Formal Powers," p. 296.

21. "Legislature to Take Up Parkland Bond Issue," *New York Times*, June 2, 1974.

22. Ira Sharkansky, "State Administrators in the Political Process," p. 251.

23. Lyman Bryson, "Notes on a Theory of Advice."

24. Samuel C. Patterson, "The Political Cultures of the American States," p. 28.

25. P. H. Burch, Jr., "Interest Groups," p. 93.

26. Reichley, "Political Containment of Cities," p. 187.

27. *Trenton Evening Times*, October 25, 1972, p. 19.

28. Authorizing legislation for the second Green Acres bond issue makes this explicit: "The most critical need for open space now exists in the urban sections of the state. Special attention should be focused on the provision of lands [in urban areas]," NJSA 13:8A-20 (e).

29. *Special aid city* is a statutory definition of a city in the state that is entitled to money from the state general fund to aid in maintaining municipal services (Laws of 1971, chap. 64). The list of special aid cities is used by various departments of the state government to identify urban problem areas. Criteria for inclusion in the category include: (1) population greater than fifteen thousand; (2) number of children receiving Aid to Dependent Children greater than 350; (3) presence of publicly financed housing; (4) a municipal equalized tax rate greater than the statewide equalized tax rate; and (5) a municipal equalized valuation per capita less than statewide equalized valuation per capita.

30. NJSA 13:8A-19.

31. For example, see the concluding chapter of the Governor's Commission to Evaluate the Capital Needs of New Jersey, *A Capital Program*.

32. Wolf, interview.

33. "An Urban-Rural Squabble Brews over Green Acres," *New York Times*, December 9, 1974.

34. Freeman, *Political Process*, pp. 62–63, suggests that at the federal level the formal powers of the executive may be sufficient to circumscribe the policy-making autonomy of the bureaucratic decision makers under him, but that exercise of formal powers alone are insufficient to produce strong policy direction from the top. This seems to apply as well to public open space policy making in New Jersey. Freeman goes on to suggest that, for strong top-level policy guidance to take place, the executive must stock the bureaucracy with enough people sympathetic with his view to infuse the bureau's "intimate environment" with that point of view. Such stocking has not taken place in the Green Acres Program.

35. Kraml, interview.

36. Chester Barnard, *The Functions of the Executive*, p. 165.

37. Simon, Smithburg, and Thompson, *Public Administration*, p. 184.

38. Willbern, "States as Components," p. 79.

39. Francis, *Legislative Issues*, p. 42.

40. John Bachalis, interview.

41. Altshuler, *City Planning Process*, p. 365, found a similar favorable disposition on the part of labor toward public projects in Minneapolis and St. Paul; and, as in the case with the Green Acres Program, as prospects for new jobs increased, so did labor's enthusiasm.

42. "Realignment of Trail Sparks Opposition," *New York Times*, March 17, 1977.

43. See, for example, *Star-Ledger*, series of articles critical of the Green Acres Program, written by F. Gregory and appearing between October 23, 1966 and November 1, 1966; or "Parkland—the Battle Goes On," *New York Times*, September 19, 1976.

44. Tannenbaum, "Preservation of Open Space," pp. 179–183.

45. Charles M. Hardin, "Observations on Environmental Politics," p. 180.

46. The preservationists and conservationists cannot be simply categorized as upper class and upper-middle class in their social status. Although Harry, Gale, and Hendee, "Conservation," have shown that some conservation groups, including the Sierra Club, have memberships strongly skewed toward the upper end of the socioeconomic scale, some groups do not. For example, the National Wildlife Foundation, which joins the other conservation groups in a united front on many issues, has a membership composed largely of working-class sportsmen who are members of the National Wildlife Federation through their affiliated local hunting or fishing clubs.

47. Briavel Holcomb, "Environmental Quality and Leadership in Northern New Jersey."

48. Ibid.

49. P. H. Burch, Jr., "Interest Groups," p. 101.

50. Sullivan, interview.

51. Ibid.

52. Which is the hand and which is the instrument is not always clear, however. Although the New Jersey Conservation Foundation recently made a major purchase on behalf of the state on receipt of a letter of intent, the tract in question was one that the foundation thought should be in public ownership, and it lobbied hard to get the state to write the letter of intent in the first place.

53. Robert Alan Dahl, *Who Governs?*, p. 156.

54. P. H. Burch, Jr., "Interest Groups," pp. 95–96.

55. Sullivan, interview.

56. Ibid.

57. *Star-Ledger*, various articles by F. Gregory, appearing between October 23, 1966 and November 1, 1966.

58. Lock, interview.

59. Kraml, interview.

60. Simon, Smithburg, and Thompson, *Public Administration*, pp. 393–394.

61. NJSA 13:8A-20 (e).

62. Emmette S. Redford, *Democracy in the Administrative State*, suggests

that, in the modern state, a great deal of administrative discretion is probably inevitable in most policy areas. Moreover, such discretion is probably preferable to hemming in administrators with an excess of regulations and restraints, which would inhibit their ability to address new problems.

63. Gregory Bateson, *Steps to an Ecology of the Mind*.

7. Conclusion

1. Many works touching on public open space have emphasized the range of disparate entities the term *open space* covers and the array of ends that open space policy can be used to pursue. Among the more recent of these works are Robert G. Healy and John S. Rosenberg, *Land Use and the States*; Eckbo, *Public Landscape*.

2. Aaron B. Wildavsky, *The Revolt against the Masses*, p. 8.

3. Healy and Rosenberg, *Land Use and the States*, p. 199, make this point by citing a 1974 study that suggested that acquiring all the land in California that ought to be left as public open space would cost $4 billion. They add that by 1979 the figure was perhaps twice that.

4. Ibid., p. 253.

5. Hall, *Land Use Planning*, p. 95.

6. Ibid.

7. Sharkansky, *Routines of Politics*, pp. 122–123.

8. U.S. Department of Commerce, Bureau of the Census, *1970 Census of Housing, Housing Characteristics for States, Cities and Counties*.

9. New Jersey Department of Environmental Protection, *Spruce Run Visitor Survey*, 1976.

10. Eagleton Institute of Politics, *New Jersey Poll, No. 7*. The total sample size was 1,051 respondents. The questions were designed by James E. Applegate, Associate Professor of Forestry, Rutgers University. The survey was conducted for the New Jersey Division of Fish, Game, and Shellfisheries.

11. It does not appear that this prevalence of what are commonly considered elite values is a uniquely local phenomenon. Studies conducted in Buffalo, Philadelphia, and Michigan indicate that support for environmental and preservationist goals is strong at all levels of society. The Environmental Studies Center of the State University of New York at Buffalo found in Buffalo that support was strong among all social strata. This study was cited in *Conservation News* 42 (1977): 211–213. F. Buttell and W. Flinn, *The Structure of Support for the Environmental Movement*, found a similar attitude in Michigan. U. Scherer and R. Coughlin, *A Pilot Household Survey of Perception and Use of a Large Urban Park*, found that a large urban park in Philadelphia was most valued by its users, who were city dwellers of greatly varying socioeconomic characteristics, for nature-oriented uses.

12. Bernard C. Hennessey, *Public Opinion*, p. 99.

13. See Melvin M. Webber, "Relations between the Social-Physical Environment of Outdoor Recreation and Mental-Physical Health," pp. 243–250, for a summary of attitudes and opinions.

14. Hennessey, *Public Opinion*, pp. 248–251.
15. Lewis Lipsitz, "On Political Belief, the Grievances of the Poor," p. 235.
16. Elson, *Guardians of Tradition*, pp. 28–33.
17. William Dean Howells, *The Landlord at Lions Head.*
18. David Harvey, *Social Justice and the City*, p. 202.
19. Denton E. Morrison, "The Environmental Movement."
20. Raymond Williams, *The Country and the City*, pp. 293–294.
21. Ibid.
22. Stillman, *Storm King Controversy*, p. 2.
23. Sam Bass Warner, *The Private City.*
24. Donald E. Simon, "A Prospect for Parks."
25. Long, "Power and Administration," p. 9.
26. Ibid., p. 10.
27. Edward C. Banfield, "Ends and Means in Planning."
28. Bryan R. Fry and Richard F. Winters, "The Politics of Redistribution."
29. Downs, *Inside Bureaucracy*, p. 216.

Bibliography

This is not a complete bibliography of open space policy making
or related fields.

Allison, Graham T. "Bureaucratic Politics." In *Bureaucratic Power in National Politics*, 2d ed., edited by Francis E. Rourke, pp. 223–240. Boston: Little, Brown, 1972.

Altshuler, Alan. *The City Planning Process: A Political Analysis.* Ithaca, N.Y.: Cornell University Press, 1965.

Bachrach, Peter, and Baratz, Morton S. "Two Faces of Power." *American Political Science Review*, December 1962, pp. 947–952.

Banfield, Edward C. "Ends and Means in Planning." In *A Reader in Planning Theory*, edited by Andreas Faludi, pp. 139–149. Oxford: Pergamon, 1973.

Banovetz, James M. *Managing the Modern City.* Washington, D.C.: International City Management Association, 1971.

Barbour, Ian G., ed. *Western Man and Environmental Ethics: Attitudes toward Nature and Technology.* Reading, Mass.: Addison-Wesley, 1973.

Barnard, Chester. *The Functions of the Executive.* 2d ed. Cambridge, Mass.: Harvard University Press, 1968.

Bateson, Gregory. *Steps to an Ecology of the Mind: Collected Essays in Anthropology, Psychiatry, Evolution and Epistemology.* San Francisco: Chandler, 1972.

Bauer, Raymond Augustine; Poole, Ithiel deSola; and Dexter, Lewis Anthony. *American Business and Public Policy.* 2d ed. Chicago: Aldine-Atherton, 1972.

Beckman, Norman. "The Planner as a Bureaucrat." In *A Reader in Planning Theory*, edited by Andreas Faludi, pp. 251–263. Oxford: Pergamon, 1973.

Bentley, Arthur F. *The Process of Government.* 2d ed. Bloomington, Ind.: Principia, 1949.

Benveniste, Guy. *The Politics of Expertise.* Berkeley, Calif.: Glendessary, 1972.

Berry, David. "Preservation of Open Space and the Concept of Value." *American Journal of Economics and Sociology* 35 (1976): 113–124.

Beyle, Thad L. "The Governor's Formal Powers: A View from the Governor's Chair." In *Comparative State Politics: A Reader*, edited by Donald P. Sprengle, pp. 292–299. Columbus, Ohio: Charles E. Merrill, 1971.

Blalock, Hubert M., Jr. *Social Statistics.* 2d ed. New York: McGraw-Hill, 1972.

Blau, Peter Michael. *The Dynamics of Bureaucracy*. Rev. ed. Chicago: University of Chicago Press, 1963.

Blydenburgh, John. "Party Organizations." In *Politics in New Jersey*, edited by Alan Rosenthal and John Blydenburgh, pp. 110–137. New Brunswick, N.J.: Eagleton Institute of Politics, 1975.

Brower, Sidney, and Williamson, Penelope. "Outdoor Recreation as a Function of the Urban Housing Environment." *Environment and Behavior*, September 1974, pp. 295–345.

Bryson, Lyman. "Notes on a Theory of Advice." *Political Science Quarterly* 66 (1951): 321–329.

Burch, Philip H., Jr. "Interest Groups." In *Politics in New Jersey*, edited by Alan Rosenthal and John Blydenburgh, pp. 81–109. New Brunswick, N.J.: Eagleton Institute of Politics, 1975.

Burch, William R. *Daydreams and Nightmares*. New York: Harper & Row, 1971.

Buttell, F., and Flinn, W. "The Structure of Support for the Environmental Movement: 1968–1970." Mimeographed. 1973.

Carhart, Arthur Hawthorne. "Historical Development of Outdoor Recreation." In *Outdoor Recreation Literature: A Survey*, ORRRC Study Report, no. 27, edited by the Outdoor Recreation Resources Review Commission, pp. 99–129. Washington, D.C.: U.S. Government Printing Office, 1962.

California, state of. *California Public Outdoor Recreation Plan*, pt. 1. Sacramento, 1960.

Campbell, Alan K., ed. *The States and the Urban Crisis*. Englewood Cliffs, N.J.: Prentice-Hall, 1970.

Campbell, Alan K., and Shalala, Donna E. "Problems Unsolved, Solutions Untried: The Urban Crisis." In *The States and the Urban Crisis*, edited by Alan K. Campbell, pp. 4–26. Englewood Cliffs, N.J.: Prentice-Hall, 1970.

Caro, Robert A. *The Power Broker: Robert Moses and the Fall of New York*. New York: Knopf, 1974.

Catlin, George. "An Artist Proposes a National Park." In *The American Environment: Readings in the History of Conservation*, edited by Roderick Nash, pp. 5–9. Reading, Mass.: Addison-Wesley, 1967.

Chadwick, George F. *The Park and the Town*. New York: Praeger, 1966.

Chandler, Robert. *Public Opinion; Changing Attitudes on Contemporary Political and Social Issues*. New York: Bowker, 1972.

Chapin, F. Stuart, Jr. *Urban Land Use Planning*. 2d ed. Urbana, Ill.: University of Illinois Press, 1972.

Citizens Conference on State Legislature. *State Legislatures: An Evaluation of Their Effectiveness*. New York: Praeger, 1971.

Clawson, Marion. "Open (Uncovered) Space as New Urban Resource." In *The Quality of the Urban Environment*, edited by Harvey S. Perloff, pp. 139–175. Baltimore: Johns Hopkins University Press (for Resources for the Future), 1969.

Clawson, Marion; Held, R. Burnell; and Stoddard, C. H. *Land for the Future*. Baltimore: Johns Hopkins University Press (for Resources for the Future), 1960.

Clawson, Marion, and Knetsch, Jack L. *Economics of Outdoor Recreation*. Baltimore: Johns Hopkins University Press (for Resources for the Future), 1966.

Clepper, Henry. *Origins of American Conservation*. New York: Ronald, 1966.

———. *Professional Forestry in the United States*. Baltimore: Johns Hopkins University Press (for Resources for the Future), 1971.

Colman, William G. *Cities, Suburbs, and States*. New York: Free Press, 1975.

Committee on Regional Plan of New York and Its Environs. *Regional Plan of New York and Its Environs*. New York, 1928.

———. *Regional Survey*. New York, 1928.

Council of State Governments. *State Responsibility in Urban Regional Development: A Report to the Governor's Conference*. Chicago, 1962.

Crozier, Michel. *The Bureaucratic Phenomenon*. Chicago: University of Chicago Press, 1964.

Dahl, Robert Alan. *Who Governs? Democracy and Power in an American City*. New Haven, Conn.: Yale University Press, 1961.

Dana, Samuel Trask. *Forest and Range Policy, Its Development in the United States*. New York: McGraw-Hill, 1956.

Daneker, L. "How Much Public Support Is There for Pollution Control? More Than You Think!" *Conservation News*, October 15, 1977, p. 3.

Dixon, W. J., ed. *Biomedical Computer Programs*. Berkeley and Los Angeles: University of California Press, 1969.

Dobriner, William Mann. *Class in Suburbia*. Englewood Cliffs, N.J.: Prentice-Hall, 1964.

Downs, Anthony. *Inside Bureaucracy*. Boston: Little, Brown, 1967.

Dunn, Diana R. "Leisure Resources in America's Inner Cities." *Parks and Recreation*, March 1974.

Dunshire, Andrew. *Implementation in a Bureaucracy*. New York: St. Martin's, 1978.

Dye, Thomas R. "Executive Power and Public Policy in the United States." In *Dimensions of State and Urban Policy Making*, edited by Richard H. Leach and Timothy G. O'Rourke, pp. 115–133. New York: Macmillan, 1975.

Eagleton Institute of Politics, Rutgers University. *New Jersey Poll, No. 2*. New Brunswick, N.J., February 1972.

———. *New Jersey Poll, No. 5*. New Brunswick, N.J., January 1973.

———. *New Jersey Poll, No. 7*. New Brunswick, N.J., May 1973.

———. *New Jersey Poll, No. 11*. New Brunswick, N.J., May 1974.

Eckbo, Garrett. *Public Landscape: Six Essays in Government and Environmental Design in the San Francisco Bay Area*. Berkeley: Institute of Governmental Studies, University of California, 1978.

Edelman, Murray. *The Symbolic Uses of Power*. Urbana, Ill.: University of Illinois Press, 1964.

Elazar, Daniel J. "The States and the Nation." In *Politics in the American States: A Comparative Analysis*, edited by Herbert Jacob and Kenneth N. Vines. Boston: Little, Brown, 1965.

Eliade, Mircea. *Cosmos and History: The Myth of the Eternal Return*. New York: Harper & Row, 1959.

Elson, Ruth Miller. *Guardians of Tradition: American Schoolbooks of the Nineteenth Century*. Lincoln: University of Nebraska Press, 1964.

Ervin, David R.; Fitch, James B.; Godwin, Kenneth R.; Shepard, W. Bruce; and Stoevener, Herbert H. *Land Use Control*. Cambridge, Mass.: Ballinger, 1977.

Faludi, Andreas, ed. *A Reader in Planning Theory*. Oxford: Pergamon, 1973.

Fox, Douglas M. *The Politics of City and State Bureaucracy*. Pacific Palisades, Calif.: Goodyear, 1974.

Francis, Wayne L. *Legislative Issues in the Fifty States: A Comparative Analysis*. Chicago: Rand-McNally, 1967.

Freeman, J. Leiper. *The Political Process: Executive Bureau–Legislative Committee Relations*. Rev. ed. New York: Random House, 1965.

Fry, Bryan R., and Winters, Richard F. "The Politics of Redistribution." *American Political Science Review*, June 1970, pp. 508–522.

Galantowicz, Richard E. *Natural Resource Systems: A New Basis for Shaping the Redevelopment of Newark*. Morristown, N.J.: New Jersey Conservation Foundation, 1975.

Gallion, Arthur B., and Eisner, Simon. *The Urban Pattern: City Planning and Design*. New York: Van Nostrand Reinhold, 1963.

Gans, Herbert J. *The Levittowners: Ways of Life and Politics in a New Suburban Community*. New York: Pantheon, 1967.

Gordon, Morton. "Ecology as Ideology." In *Environmental Quality and Society*, edited by Richard A. Tybout, pp. 59–69. Columbus, Ohio: Ohio State University Press, 1975.

Gore, William J. "Decision-making Research: Some Prospects and Limitations." In *Concepts and Issues in Administrative Behavior*, edited by Sidney Mailick and Edward H. Van Ness, pp. 49–65. Englewood Cliffs, N.J.: Prentice-Hall, 1962.

Gottmann, Jean. *Megalopolis: The Urbanized Northeastern Seaboard of the United States*. New York: Twentieth Century Fund, 1961.

Governor's Commission to Evaluate the Capital Needs of New Jersey. *A Capital Program*. Trenton, 1968.

Governor's Pinelands Review Committee. *Planning and Management of the New Jersey Pinelands*. Trenton, 1979.

Graber, Linda. *Wilderness as Sacred Space*. Washington, D.C.: Association of American Geographers, 1976.

Graham, Frank, Jr. *The Adirondack Park: A Political History*. New York: Knopf, 1978.

Grodzins, Morton. "The Many American Governments and Outdoor Recreation." In *Trends in American Living and Outdoor Recreation*, ORRRC Study Report, No. 22, edited by the Outdoor Recreation Resources Review Commission, pp. 61–80. Washington, D.C.: U.S. Government Printing Office, 1962.

Hall, Thomas. "Land Use Planning and Management, the Role of State Government." Ph.D. dissertation, Rutgers University, 1975.

Hanmer, Lee Franklin. *Public Recreation, Parks, Playgrounds and Outdoor Recre-*

ation Facilities. Vol. 5 in *Regional Survey,* Committee on Regional Plan of New York and Its Environs. New York, 1928.

Hardin, Charles M. "Observations on Environmental Politics." In *Environmental Politics,* edited by Stuart S. Nagel, pp. 177–194. New York: Praeger, 1974.

Harry, Joseph; Gale, Richard F.; and Hendee, John C. "Conservation: An Upper-middle Class Social Movement." *Journal of Leisure Research* 1 (1969): 246–254.

Harvey, David. *Social Justice and the City.* Baltimore: Johns Hopkins University Press, 1973.

———. "Social Process and Spatial Form: An Analysis of the Conceptual Problems of Urban Planning." In *Readings in Social Geography,* edited by Emrys Jones, pp. 288–306. London: Oxford University Press, 1975.

Haskell, Elizabeth H., and Price, Victoria S. *State Environmental Management.* New York: Praeger, 1973.

Healy, Robert G., and Rosenberg, John S. *Land Use and the States.* 2d ed. Baltimore: Johns Hopkins University Press (for Resources for the Future), 1979.

Heckscher, August. *Open Spaces: The Life of American Cities,* New York: Harper & Row, 1977.

Hennessey, Bernard C. *Public Opinion.* 3d ed. North Scituate, Mass.: Duxbury, 1975.

Hill, Michael J. *The Sociology of Public Administration.* New York: Crane, Russak, 1972.

Hirschman, Albert O. *Exit, Voice and Loyalty: Responses to Decline in Firms, Organizations and States.* Cambridge, Mass.: Harvard University Press, 1970.

Holcomb, Briavel. "Environmental Quality and Leadership in Northern New Jersey: An Exploratory Investigation." Mimeograph. New Brunswick, N.J.: Rutgers University, 1974.

Howells, William Dean. *The Landlord at Lions Head.* New York: Harper & Brothers, 1897.

Huth, Hans. *Nature and the American.* Berkeley and Los Angeles: University of California Press, 1957.

Ise, John. *Our National Park Policy: A Critical History.* Baltimore: Johns Hopkins University Press (for Resources for the Future), 1961.

Jacob, Herbert, and Vines, Kenneth N. *Politics in the American States, a Comparative Analysis.* Boston: Little, Brown, 1965.

Jacobs, Jane. *The Death and Life of Great American Cities.* New York: Modern Library, 1969.

Jensen, Clayne R. *Outdoor Recreation in America: Trends, Problems and Opportunities.* 3d ed. Minneapolis: Burgess, 1978.

Johnson, Robert Underwood. "Aesthetics and Conservation." In *The American Environment: Readings in the History of Conservation,* 2d ed., edited by Roderick Nash, pp. 68–71. Reading, Mass.: Addison-Wesley, 1976.

Jones, Bryan D. "Distributional Considerations in Models of Government Service Provision." *Urban Affairs Quarterly*, March 1977, pp. 291–312.

Knapp, Richard F. "Play for America, pt. I: Municipal Recreation: Background of an Era." *Parks and Recreation*, August 1972.

Kolesar, John N. "The States and Urban Planning and Development." In *The States and the Urban Crisis*, edited by Alan K. Campbell, pp. 114–135. Englewood Cliffs, N.J.: Prentice-Hall, 1970.

Leach, Richard H., and O'Rourke, Timothy G., eds. *Dimensions of State and Urban Policy Making*. New York: Macmillan, 1975.

League of Women Voters. *New Jersey: Spotlight on Government*. North Plainfield, N.J.: Twin Cities Press, 1969.

Lee, J. "State Legislative Decision-making." In *Dimensions of State and Urban Policy Making*, edited by Richard H. Leach and Timothy G. O'Rourke, pp. 156–175. New York: Macmillan, 1975.

Leff, Herbert L. *Experience, Environment and Human Potentials*. New York: Oxford University Press, 1978.

Lehne, Richard. "Revenue and Expenditure Policies." In *Politics in New Jersey*, edited by Alan Rosenthal and John Blydenburgh, pp. 243–271. New Brunswick, N.J.: Eagleton Institute of Politics, 1975.

Levitt, Morris J., and Feldbaum, Eleanor G. *State and Local Government and Politics*. Hinsdale, Ill.: Dryden, 1973.

Levy, Frank; Meltsner, Arnold J.; and Wildavsky, Aaron B. *Urban Outcomes*. Berkeley and Los Angeles: University of California Press, 1974.

Lineberry, Robert. *Equality and Urban Policy*. Beverly Hills, Calif.: Sage, 1977.

Linowes, Robert R., and Allensworth, Don T. *The Politics of Land Use: Planning, Zoning and the Private Developer*. New York: Praeger, 1973.

Lipset, Seymour Martin; Trow, Martin A.; and Coleman, James S. *Union Democracy: The Internal Politics of the International Typographical Union*. Glencoe, Ill.: Free Press, 1956.

Lipsitz, Lewis. "On Political Belief, the Grievances of the Poor." In *Public Opinion and Political Attitudes*, edited by Allen R. Wilcox, pp. 272–287. New York: Wiley, 1974.

Little, Charles E. *The Challenge of Land*. New York: Pergamon, 1968.

———. "Preservation Policy and Personal Perception: A 200 Million Acre Misunderstanding." In *Landscape Assessment: Values, Perceptions and Resources*, edited by Ervin H. Zube, Robert O. Brush, and Julius Fabos, pp. 46–57. Stroudsburg, Pa.: Dowden, Hutchinson, & Ross, 1975.

Long, Norton E. "Power and Administration." In *Bureaucratic Power in National Politics*, 2d ed., edited by Francis E. Rourke, pp. 5–14. Boston: Little, Brown, 1972.

Lowi, Theodore. "American Business and Public Policy: Case Studies and Political Theory." *World Politics* 16 (1964): 677–715.

Lynn, K. "Neighborhood Commons." *Architectural Design*, August 1964, pp. 42–46.

Maass, Arthur. "Areal Division of Power." In *Area and Power: A Theory of Local Government*, edited by Arthur Maass, pp. 9–26. Glencoe, Ill.: Free Press, 1959.

Mailick, Sidney, and Van Ness, Edward H., eds. *Concepts and Issues in Administrative Behavior.* Englewood Cliffs, N.J.: Prentice-Hall, 1972.

March, James G., and Simon, Herbert A. *Organizations.* New York: Wiley, 1958.

Marx, Leo. "Pastoral Ideals and City Troubles." In *Western Man and Environmental Ethics: Attitudes toward Nature and Technology,* edited by Ian G. Barbour, pp. 93–115. Reading, Mass.: Addison-Wesley, 1973.

Massachusetts Department of Natural Resources. *Making Massachusetts a Better Place to Live, Work and Play.* Boston, 1958.

McCormick, Jack. *The Pine Barrens: A Preliminary Ecological Inventory.* New

McCormick, Jack, and Jones, Leslie. *The Pine Barrens: A Vegetation Geography.* New Jersey State Museum Research Report, No. 3. Trenton, 1973.

McHarg, Ian. *Design with Nature.* Garden City, N.Y.: Doubleday, 1971.

McPhee, John. *The Pine Barrens.* New York: Farrar, Straus & Giroux, 1968.

Minnesota Department of Conservation. *Land, Land Use and Recreation.* Minneapolis, 1960.

Moncrief, L. "The Cultural Basis of Our Environmental Crisis." In *Western Man and Environmental Ethics: Attitudes toward Nature and Technology,* edited by Ian G. Barbour, pp. 31–42. Reading, Mass.: Addison-Wesley, 1973.

Morrison, Denton E. "The Environmental Movement: Some Preliminary Observations and Predictions." In *Social Behavior, Natural Resources, and the Environment,* edited by William R. Burch, Jr., Neil H. Cheek, Jr., and Lee Taylor, pp. 259–279. New York: Harper & Row, 1972.

Mueller, Eva, and Gurin, Gerald. *Participation in Outdoor Recreation: Factors Affecting Demand among American Adults.* ORRRC Study Report, No. 20. Washington, D.C.: U.S. Government Printing Office, 1962.

Muir, John. *Our National Parks.* Boston: Houghton, 1901.

Mumford, Lewis. "Constancy and Change." *New Yorker,* March 6, 1965, pp. 158–170.

Nagel, Stuart S., ed. *Environmental Politics.* New York: Praeger, 1974.

Nash, Roderick. *Wilderness and the American Mind.* New Haven, Conn.: Yale University Press, 1967.

———, ed. *The American Environment: Readings in the History of Conservation.* 2d ed. Reading, Mass.: Addison-Wesley, 1976.

Needleman, Martin L., and Needleman, Carolyn Emerson. *Guerrillas in the Bureaucracy.* New York: Wiley, 1974.

New Jersey Commission of Investigation. *Seventh Annual Report.* Trenton, June 1976.

New Jersey Department of Community Affairs, Division of State and Regional Planning. *New Jersey Municipal Profiles: Intensity of Urbanization.* Trenton, 1972.

———. "Statewide Comprehensive Outdoor Recreation Plan." Draft version. Trenton, 1977.

New Jersey Department of Conservation and Economic Development. *Report on Land Use Planning.* Trenton, 1959.

——. *The Need for a State Recreation Land Acquisition and Development Program.* Trenton, 1960.

——, Bureau of State and Regional Planning. *Development Plan for New Jersey.* Trenton, 1951.

——, Division of State and Regional Planning. *Setting for the New Jersey Development Plan.* Trenton, 1966.

——. *New Jersey Open Space Policy Plan.* Trenton, 1967.

——. *Statewide Comprehensive Outdoor Recreation Plan.* Trenton, 1967.

New Jersey Department of Environmental Protection. *Administrative Order No. 15.* September 13, 1971.

——. *Spruce Run Visitor Survey.* Trenton, 1976.

——. "Green Acres Quarterly Summary of Completed and Active Projects." Unpublished document. Trenton, April 1977.

——. *Establishing Green Belts and Parks: A Case History of New Jersey's Green Acres Program.* Trenton, n.d.

——. "General Policy Statements: Green Acres Development and Acquisition." Unpublished document. Trenton, n.d.

——. Division of Parks, Forestry and Recreation. *New Jersey Open Space Recreation Plan.* Trenton, n.d.

New Jersey Pinelands Commission. *Draft Comprehensive Management Plan.* New Lisbon, N.J., 1980.

New Jersey State Legislature, Office of Fiscal Affairs. *The New Jersey Green Acres Land Acquisition Program.* Division of Program Analysis Report, No. 6. Trenton, 1975.

New Jersey State Planning Board. *Where Shall We Play?: A Report on the Outdoor Recreation Needs of New Jersey.* Trenton, 1938.

——. *Parks and Public Lands in New Jersey.* Trenton, 1941.

New York Department of Conservation. *Now or Never.* Albany, 1960.

Nienaber, Jeanne, and Wildavsky, Aaron B. *The Budgeting and Evaluation of Federal Recreation Programs: Or, Money Doesn't Grow on Trees.* New York: Basic Books, 1973.

Niering, William A. *Nature in the Metropolis.* RPA Bulletin, No. 95. New York: Regional Plan Association, 1960.

O'Brien, Raymond. "The Role of Highland Aesthetics in the Creation of an Interstate Park: Geographic Conception in the Lower Hudson Valley and the Evolution of a Regional Recreation Landscape." Ph.D. dissertation, Rutgers University, 1975.

O'Connor, James R. *The Fiscal Crisis of the State.* New York: St. Martin's, 1973.

Olmsted, Frederick Law. *Civilizing American Cities: A Selection of Frederick Law Olmsted's Writings on City Landscapes.* Edited by S. B. Sutton. Cambridge, Mass.: M.I.T. Press, 1971.

——. "The Value and Care of Parks." In *The American Environment: Readings in the History of Conservation,* 2d ed., edited by Roderick Nash, pp. 18–24. Reading, Mass.: Addison-Wesley, 1976.

Outdoor Recreation Resources Review Commission. *Outdoor Recreation for*

America. Washington, D.C.: U.S. Government Printing Office, 1962.

———, ed. *Outdoor Recreation Literature: A Survey*. ORRRC Study Report, No. 27. Washington, D.C.: U.S. Government Printing Office, 1962.

———, ed. *Trends in American Living and Outdoor Recreation*. ORRRC Study Report, No. 22. Washington, D.C.: U.S. Government Printing Office, 1962.

Pahl, Raymond E. *Whose City? And Other Essays in Sociology and Planning*. London: Harlow, Longman, 1970.

Patterson, Samuel C. "The Political Cultures of the American States." In *Comparative State Politics: A Reader*, edited by Donald P. Sprengle, pp. 12–33. Columbus, Ohio: Charles E. Merrill, 1971.

Peffer, E. Louise. *The Closing of the Public Domain: Disposal and Reservation Policies, 1900–1950*. New York: Arno, 1972.

Perloff, Harvey S., ed. *The Quality of the Urban Environment*. Baltimore: Johns Hopkins University Press (for Resources for the Future), 1969.

Platt, Rutherford H. *The Open Space Decision Process: Spatial Allocation of Costs and Benefits*. Chicago: Department of Geography, University of Chicago, 1972.

Poland, Orville F. "Planning as a Function of Public Administration and Evaluation." In *Program Evaluation in the Public Sector*, edited by Albert C. Hyde and Jay M. Shafrit, pp. 199–209. New York: Praeger, 1979.

Pressman, Jeffrey L., and Wildavsky, Aaron B. *Implementation: How Great Expectations in Washington Are Dashed in Oakland, etc*. Berkeley and Los Angeles: University of California Press, 1973.

Presthus, Robert J. "Authority in Organizations." In *Concepts and Issues in Administrative Behavior*, edited by Sidney Mailick and Edward H. Van Ness, pp. 122–136. Englewood Cliffs, N.J.: Prentice-Hall, 1962.

Queale and Lynch, Inc. "Urban State Parks Study." Unpublished report to the New Jersey Department of Community Affairs, Division of State and Regional Planning. September 1972.

Rabinovitz, Francine F. "Politics, Personality and Planning." In *A Reader in Planning Theory*, edited by Andreas Faludi, pp. 265–276. Oxford: Pergamon, 1973.

Redford, Emmette S. *Democracy in the Administrative State*. New York: Oxford University Press, 1969.

———. *Ideal and Practice in Public Administration*. University: University of Alabama Press, 1958.

Regional Plan Association. *The Race for Open Space: Final Report of the Park, Recreation and Open Space Project*. RPA Bulletin, No. 96. New York, 1960.

———. *Spread City*. RPA Bulletin, No. 100, New York, 1962.

Reichley, A. James. "The Political Containment of Cities." In *The States and the Urban Crisis*, edited by Alan K. Campbell, pp. 169–195. Englewood Cliffs, N.J.: Prentice-Hall, 1970.

Richardson, Elmo. *Dams, Parks and Politics: Resource Development and Preservation in the Truman-Eisenhower Era*. Lexington: University of Kentucky Press, 1973.

Rosenthal, Alan. "The Governor, the Legislature and State Policy Making." In *Politics in New Jersey*, edited by Alan Rosenthal and John Blydenburgh, pp. 141–174. New Brunswick, N.J.: Eagleton Institute of Politics, 1975.

Rosenthal, Alan, and Blydenburgh, John, eds. *Politics in New Jersey*. New Brunswick, N.J.: Eagleton Institute of Politics, 1975.

Rourke, Francis E. "Variations in Agency Power." In *Bureaucratic Power in National Politics*, 2d ed., edited by Francis E. Rourke, pp. 240–262. Boston: Little, Brown, 1972.

———, ed. *Bureaucratic Power in National Politics*. 2d ed. Boston: Little, Brown, 1972.

Sax, J. "Our National Parks." *Natural History Magazine*, October 1976, pp. 57–88.

Scherer, U., and Coughlin, R. *A Pilot Household Survey of Perception and Use of a Large Urban Park*. Regional Science Research Institute Discussion Paper, Series No. 59. Philadelphia: Regional Science Research Institute, 1976.

Schiff, Ashley. *Fire and Water: Scientific Heresy in the Forest Service*. Cambridge, Mass.: Harvard University Press, 1962.

Schlesinger, Joseph A. "The Politics of the Executive." In *Politics in the American States, a Comparative Analysis*, edited by Herbert Jacob and Kenneth N. Vines, pp. 210–237. Boston: Little, Brown, 1965.

Sharkansky, Ira. *The Routines of Politics*. New York: Van Nostrand Reinhold, 1970.

———. "State Administrators in the Political Process." In *Politics in the American States, a Comparative Analysis*, edited by Herbert Jacob and Kenneth N. Vines, pp. 238–271. Boston: Little, Brown, 1965.

Shepard, Paul. *Man in the Landscape: A Historic View of the Esthetics of Nature*. New York: Ballantine, 1967.

Sills, David. "The Environmental Movement and Its Critics." *Human Ecology* 3 (1975): 1–40.

Simon, Donald E. "A Prospect for Parks." *Public Interest*, Summer 1976, pp. 27–39.

Simon, Herbert A.; Smithburg, Donald W.; and Thompson, Victor A. *Public Administration*. New York: Knopf, 1950.

Slatterthwaite, Ann, and Marcou, George T. "Planning Open Space." In *Principles and Practices of Urban Planning*, 4th ed., edited by William I. Goodman, pp. 188–199. Washington, D.C.: International City Managers Association, 1968.

Smith, David Marshall. *The Geography of Social Well Being in the United States*. New York: McGraw-Hill, 1973.

Smith, Edward Ellis, and Riggs, Durward S. *Land Use, Open Space and the Government Process*. New York: Praeger, 1974.

Smith, Wallace F. "Filtering and Neighborhood Change." In *Internal Structure of the City*. edited by Larry S. Bourne, pp. 170–179. New York: Oxford University Press, 1971.

Sprengle, Donald P., ed. *Comparative State Politics: A Reader*. Columbus, Ohio: Charles E. Merrill, 1971.

Springer, J. Fred, and Constantini, Edmond. "Public Opinion and the Environment: An Issue in Search of a Home." In *Environmental Politics*, edited by Stuart S. Nagel, pp. 195–224. New York: Praeger, 1974.

Stedman, Murray S., Jr. *Urban Politics*. 2d ed. Cambridge, Mass.: Winthrop, 1972.

Stillman, Calvin. *The Issues in the Storm King Controversy*. Black Rock Forest Paper, No. 27. Cornwall, N.Y.: Harvard Black Rock Forest, 1965.

———. "This Fair Land." In *Landscape Assessment: Values, Perceptions and Resources*, edited by Ervin H. Zube, Robert O. Brush, and Julius Fabos, pp. 18–30. Stroudsburg, Pa.: Dowden, Hutchinson, & Ross, 1975.

Strong, Ann Louise. *Private Property and the Public Interest: The Brandywine Experience*. Baltimore: Johns Hopkins University Press, 1975.

Tannenbaum, Elizabeth. "The Preservation of Open Space in Seven New York Counties." Ph.D. dissertation, Columbia University, 1965.

Tri-State Regional Planning Commission. *Outdoor Recreation in a Crowded Region: A Plan for Selecting and Acquiring Recreation Lands*. New York, 1969.

Truman, David B. *The Governmental Process*. New York: Knopf, 1951.

Tulluck, Gordon. *Politics of Bureaucracy*. Washington, D.C.: Public Affairs Press, 1965.

Tybout, Richard A. "The Two Market Biases." In *Environmental Quality and Society*, edited by Richard A. Tybout, pp. 239–259. Columbus, Ohio: Ohio State University Press, 1975.

U.S. Department of Commerce, Bureau of the Census. *1970 Census of Housing, Housing Characteristics for States, Cities and Counties*. Vol. 1, pt. 32. Washington, D.C.: U.S. Government Printing Office, 1972.

U.S. Department of Interior, Bureau of Outdoor Recreation. *Outdoor Recreation Action*. Quarterly periodical. Washington, D.C., 1966+.

———. *The New Jersey Pine Barrens: Concepts for Preservation*. Washington, D.C.: U.S. Government Printing Office, 1975.

———. "State Financial Assistance to Local Governments for Outdoor Recreation and Open Space." Unpublished document. Washington, D.C., December 1977.

Wamsley, Gary L., and Zald, Mayer W. *The Political Economy of Public Organizations: A Critical Approach to the Study of Public Administration*. Bloomington, Ind.: Indiana University Press, 1976.

Warner, Sam Bass. *Streetcar Suburbs: The Process of Growth in Boston, 1870–1900*. Cambridge, Mass.: Harvard University Press, 1964.

———. *The Private City: Philadelphia in Three Periods of Its Growth*. Philadelphia: University of Pennsylvania Press, 1968.

Webber, Melvin M. "Relations between the Social-Physical Environment of Outdoor Recreation and Mental-Physical Health: A Conference Summary." In *Trends in American Living and Outdoor Recreation*, ORRRC Study Report, No. 22, edited by Outdoor Recreation Resources Review Commission, pp. 243–250. Washington, D.C.: U.S. Government Printing Office, 1962.

———. "Comprehensive Planning and Social Responsibility: Toward an

A.I.P. Consensus on the Profession's Roles and Purposes." *Journal of the American Institute of Planners* 29 (1963): 232–241.

Weber, Max. "Bureaucracy." In *Organizations: Structure and Behavior*, vol. 1, 2d ed., edited by Joseph A. Litterer, pp. 29–39. New York: Wiley, 1969.

White, Morton Gabriel, and White, Lucia. *The Intellectual versus the City*. Cambridge, Mass.: Harvard University Press and the M.I.T. Press, 1962.

Whyte, William H. *The Last Landscape*. Garden City, N.Y.: Doubleday, 1970.

Wildavsky, Aaron B. "Aesthetic Power or the Triumph of a Sensitive Minority over the Vulgar Masses: A Political Analysis of the New Economics." *Daedalus*, no. 3 (1967), pp. 1115–1128.

———. "The Agency, Roles and Perspectives." In *Policy Making in American Government*, edited by Edward V. Schneier, pp. 78–88. New York: Basic Books, 1969.

———. *The Revolt against the Masses*. New York: Basic Books, 1971.

Willbern, York. "The States as Components in an Areal Division of Power." In *Area and Power: A Theory of Local Government*, edited by Arthur Maass, pp. 70–88. Glencoe, Ill.: Free Press, 1959.

Williams, Raymond. *The Country and the City*. New York: Oxford University Press, 1973.

Wilson, James Q., and Banfield, Edward C. "Public Regardingness as a Value Premise in Voting Behavior." In *Urban Political Analysis, a Systems Approach*, edited by David R. Morgan and Samuel A. Kirkpatrick, pp. 62–74. New York: Free Press, 1972.

Zube, Ervin H.; Brush, Robert O.; and Fabos, Julius, eds. *Landscape Assessment: Values, Perceptions and Resources*. Stroudsburg, Pa.: Dowden, Hutchinson, & Ross, 1975.

Interviews

Bachalis, John, Information Officer, New Jersey Manufacturers Association, telephone interview, July 15, 1977.

Beardsley, Edward, Supervisor, Green Acres Local Acquisition Grants Program, interview, June 15, 1977.

Blumenthal, Arthur, Green Acres Program Coordinator for the city of Newark, interview, December 17, 1976.

Burgio, Jane, New Jersey State Assemblywoman, telephone interview, September 3, 1977.

Chavooshian, Budd, former Director, New Jersey Division of State and Regional Planning, interview, July 6, 1977.

Fairbrothers, David, Professor of Botany, Rutgers University, interview, February 22, 1980.

Kraml, John, Supervisor, Design and Construction, New Jersey Bureau of Parks, interview, July 12, 1977.

Lloyd, Edward, New Jersey Public Interest Research Group, telephone interview, July 8, 1977.

Lock, Barry, Director, Hunterdon County Parks Department, interview, December 14, 1976.

Marshall, Robert, Senior Planner, Office of Pinelands Acquisition, New Jersey Department of Environmental Protection, interview, February 19, 1980.

Merrill, Leland G., Jr., Professor of Natural Resource Policy Studies, Center for Coastal and Environmental Studies, interview, February 27, 1980.

Moore, David, Executive Director, New Jersey Conservation Foundation, interview, July 18, 1977.

Nagy, Louis, Principal Planner, Office of Real Estate and Legal Services, New Jersey Department of Environmental Protection, interview, May 18, 1977.

Perry, R., Senior Planner, Green Acres Local Acquisition Grants Program, interview, June 15, 1977.

Shore, William B., Vice-president for Public Affairs, Regional Plan Association, telephone interview, July 7, 1977.

Smith, Mitchell, Senior Wildlife Biologist, New Jersey Division of Fish, Game, and Shellfisheries, interview, July 14, 1977.

Stansfield, Donald, Chief, New Jersey Bureau of Statewide Planning, interview, July 20, 1977.

Stokes, Robert, Chief of Recreation Planning, New Jersey Department of Environmental Protection, interview, July 19, 1977.

Sullivan, Richard, former Commissioner, New Jersey Department of Environmental Protection, interview, July 26, 1977.

Wolf, Howard, Director, Green Acres Local Grants Program, interview, June 15, 1976.

Index